# THE
# INCAS

# CULTURES OF THE PAST

# THE INCAS

## KATHRYN HINDS

**BENCHMARK BOOKS**

MARSHALL CAVENDISH
NEW YORK

To Judith Whipple, my editor and friend, with gratitude

And, as always, more thanks than words can express to
Mom, Dad, Arthur, and Owen

Benchmark Books
Marshall Cavendish Corporation
99 White Plains Road
Tarrytown, New York 10591-9001

**Library of Congress Cataloging-in-Publication Data**
Hinds, Kathryn.
     The Incas / by Kathryn Hinds.
          p.     cm.— (Cultures of the past)
     Includes bibliographical references and index.
     Summary: Examines the history, culture, religion, and social structure of the
ancient Incas.
     ISBN 0-7614-0270-5
     1. Incas—History—Juvenile literature. 2. Incas—Social life and customs—
Juvenile literature. [1. Incas. 2. Indians of South America.]   I. Title. II. Series.
F3429.H55     1998
985'.01—dc20                                                           96-30799

Printed in Hong Kong

Photo research by Barbara Scott

*Front cover:* Silver figure of an Inca noble
*Back cover:* Machu Picchu; the best-preserved Inca city yet rediscovered

**Photo Credits**
Front cover, pages 12 (bottom), 44, 49: Museum fur Volkerkunde, Berlin/Werner Forman
Archive/Art Resource, NY; back cover, page 70: Viesti Associates, Inc./Craig Lovell; page
6: from the Collection of The Gilcrease Museum; page 7: Woodfin Camp & Associates/
Douglas Mason; pages 10, 22, 24, 35, 68: Woodfin Camp & Associates/Mireille Vautier;
pages 12 (top), 14, 47: courtesy of the Brooklyn Museum of Art, (1995.29.11), (1995.29.14),
(1995.29.12); page 13: courtesy Department of Library Services/Beckett/American
Museum of Natural History, (neg. #338630); page 17: Stock Montage, Inc./© Newberry
Library; pages 18, 30-31, 37, 38-39, 51, 59, 60: Odyssey/Robert Frerck; page 19 (top and
bottom), 43: Woodfin Camp & Associates/Robert Frerck; page 19 (middle): The
Metropolitan Museum of Art, Gift of Nathan Cummings, 1963, (63.226.7); pages 21, 26
(top), 27, 46: American Museum of Natural History/John Bigelow Taylor, (neg. 4955), (neg.
5084), (neg. 5004), (neg. #4959); page 26 (bottom), 28, 50: Werner Forman/Art Resource,
NY; pages 29, 58: courtesy of Department of Library Services/Logan/American Museum of
Natural History, (neg. #125904), (neg. #125929), (neg. #1259331); page 32: Museum of the
American Indian, NY/ Werner Forman Archive/Art Resource, NY; page 33: The Textile
Museum, Washington, D.C. (91.743); page 53: The Metropolitan Museum of Art, Gift of
Arthur M. Bullowa, 1983, (1983.497.6); page 54-55: Woodfin Camp & Associates/Loren
McIntyre; page 61: DDB Stock Photo/D. Donne Bryant; page 63: DDB Stock Photo/
Virginia Ferrero; page 65: Brooklyn Museum of Art, Museum Expedition 1941, Frank L.
Babbott Fund, (41.1275.400); page 67: Viesti Associates/A.S.K.; page 69: Loren McIntyre;
page 71: Scott Vlaun; page 80: Cam Vuong.

# CONTENTS

# CHAPTER ONE

# THE FOUR QUARTERS OF THE WORLD

In the Andes Mountains of western South America there are peaks that tower three miles and more above sea level. At such heights there is little oxygen in the air, so breathing can be difficult for those not used to the altitude. The nights are bitter cold. Rain comes only in the spring, and then in torrents. Landslides, avalanches, and earthquakes are not uncommon. Only 2 percent of the land is farmable.

Opposite: *An Inca trail snakes through the Peruvian Andes.*

It is difficult to imagine that anyone could eke out a living in such an environment. Yet in the Andes a people called the Incas built a great civilization and an empire that they named Tahuantinsuyu (tah-WAHN-tin-SOO-yoo), "the Four Quarters of the World." At its height in the early sixteenth century, the Inca empire stretched more than 2,500 miles from what is now northern Ecuador to central Chile. Its birthplace and capital was Cuzco (KOOZ-koh), Peru.

Below: *Manco Capac, the legendary first Inca*

## The First Incas

According to legend, the ancestors of the Incas were Manco Capac (MAHN-koh KAH-pahk) and Mama Ocllo (OHK-yoh), who was Manco's sister as well as his wife. They came from Lake Titicaca (tih-tee-KAH-kuh), which is on the present border between Peru and Bolivia. The sun god had given them a golden staff, telling them that they should settle where the staff sank completely into the ground. After much wandering, Manco and Mama Ocllo reached a fertile valley. Manco threw the golden staff, and it buried itself in the earth. There he founded the city of Cuzco, whose name was said to mean "the navel of the world," and became its first ruler.

Inca legends told of the glorious deeds of Manco Capac and the kings who succeeded him. Many of the early kings were said to have been great conquerors, carrying the rule of the supremely powerful Incas to distant regions. In fact, until the early fifteenth century Cuzco was most likely little more than a village, and the Incas were only one of many warring tribes in the valley. They made raids on other villages and perhaps sometimes collected tribute from these villages, but otherwise left them alone. The days of empire were still ahead.

## The Turning Point

The first permanent conquests were probably made in the area surrounding Cuzco by the seventh ruler, Yahuar Huaca (YAH-war WAH-kuh). The Incas' domains in the Valley of Cuzco were further enlarged by Yahuar's son, who took the name Viracocha (veer-uh-KOH-chuh)—the name of the Incas' creator god. Viracocha was also the first ruler to be called the Sapa Inca, the "Unique or Supreme Inca"; this became the title for all the Inca rulers afterward.

Like many of his predecessors, Viracocha added to the Incas' power by making ties with neighboring peoples through marriage—his wife was the daughter of the chief of Anta, northwest of Cuzco. The Sapa Inca also made an alliance with the powerful Quechua (KESH-wah) people to the north. However, these allies were soon conquered by the even more powerful Chancas. The Chancas had been steadily expanding from their territory west of Cuzco, and it was only a matter of time before they would try to overrun the Inca domain.

Viracocha was an old and feeble man when the attack finally came. The Chanca force was so strong that it seemed useless to resist the invasion. Viracocha, his heir, and many nobles and warriors fled from Cuzco to safety. But one group of nobles stayed behind to defend the city. They were led by Viracocha's son Yupanqui (yoo-PAHN-kee).

Yupanqui had few troops, but he called on warriors from neighboring tribes for assistance. He was also helped, according to legend, by the very rocks on the battlefield, which turned into warriors in response to his prayers. In any case, Yupanqui's forces were able to drive back the Chancas, and Cuzco was saved.

More battles followed. When Yupanqui had finally defeated the last of the Chanca armies, the Incas found themselves to be the most powerful

The Incas had no system of writing. Much of their history was preserved in songs that were sung on special occasions to celebrate the deeds of the current ruler. When a new ruler came to the throne, he ordered new songs to be composed to celebrate his deeds, and many of the old songs were no longer allowed to be sung. However, each ruler's memory was kept alive by a special group of his descendants. It is not surprising, then, that there were many different versions of Inca history and that many facts were left out of it.

In 1532 the Inca empire was conquered by Spain. Most of what we now know about the Incas comes from Spanish soldiers, priests, and government officials, who wrote many books about the Incas in the sixteenth and seventeenth centuries. These authors drew on their own observations, reports of other observers, and the Incas' oral history. Unfortunately the information they were able to gather was frequently incomplete and contradictory. And the Spanish writers' understanding of Inca culture was often limited by their belief that European culture was superior to all others.

In addition we have two books that can be considered native sources, although the author of the first spent most of his life in Spain. This was Garcilaso de la Vega, the son of a Spanish father and an Inca mother. In 1609, toward the end of his life, he published his *Royal Commentaries of the Incas.* Garcilaso's descriptions of Inca history, religion, and customs were drawn from his memories of what he had seen and heard during his childhood and adolescence in Cuzco. However, he was so intent on inspiring admiration for his mother's people that he often exaggerated and distorted facts to better please his Spanish readers.

The other native author was Huaman Poma (WAH-mahn POH-mah), the son of a chief whose tribe had been under Inca rule for several generations. Huaman Poma spent thirty years traveling around the lands of Tahuantinsuyu, listening to people's tales of life before the conquest—and observing the hardships and injustices of Spanish rule. The result of his research was *The First New Chronicle and Good Government,* written sometime between 1567 and 1615. He sent this as a letter to the king of Spain, pleading for better treatment for his people; the king apparently never saw it, however. But Huaman Poma's book has been especially valuable to historians because the author illustrated it with hundreds of drawings—the only firsthand pictures of Inca life. Recent studies suggest that *The First New Chronicle* may actually have been written by a half-Inca, half-Spanish priest named Blas Valera. But whoever wrote and illustrated the book, it remains an important source of knowledge about the Incas.

To get a reasonably truthful portrait of the Incas, all these different sources have to be carefully compared and evaluated. In addition, the findings of archaeologists have been of immense help in sorting out the tangle of Inca history. As archaeologists continue to make new discoveries, our knowledge of the Inca empire and its people will continue to grow.

One of Pachacuti's conquests was the area along the Urubamba River, northeast of Cuzco, where the ruins of the Inca city of Pisac still stand. The Urubamba originally took a winding course through this valley, but the Sapa Inca ordered the building of canals to straighten the river.

people in the entire region. Yupanqui was hailed as a great hero. The leading nobles made him Sapa Inca in place of his father, who remained in retirement and probably died soon afterward. All this happened around the year 1438.

## The Earth Shaker

Yupanqui now took the name Pachacuti (pah-chah-KOO-tee), meaning "earth shaker" or "he who transforms the world." And Pachacuti did indeed transform the Andean world. He was the founder and organizer of the Inca empire. His policies affected every aspect of the lives of the people of his realm, and the legacy of those policies is still felt in the Andes today.

Sometime before the Chanca war, according to one story, Pachacuti had received a powerful vision. The sun god had appeared to him and told him that he would conquer many nations. With the Chancas defeated, Pachacuti set about making the prophecy come true. Under his rule, Inca armies advanced into every quarter of Tahuantinsuyu: Chinchasuyu in the north, Condesuyu in the west, Collasuyu in the south, and Antisuyu in the east.

Pachacuti personally led many of the campaigns. He conquered the area northwest of Cuzco almost all the way to the source of the Huallaga (wy-YAH-gah) River, one of the tributaries of the Amazon. Roughly 650 miles away in Collasuyu, he reached the ancient city of Tiahuanaco (tee-uh-wuh-NAH-koh) on the southeastern shore of Lake Titicaca.

Some of Pachacuti's conquests were made without bloodshed. The Sapa Inca would send ambassadors to the people he wanted to conquer. These ambassadors would describe all of the advantages of becoming part of the Inca empire. One of the greatest advantages, of course, was not having to go to war against the Incas, who had gained a fearsome reputation. In this way many Andean tribes were peacefully persuaded to accept the Sapa Inca's authority.

## INCA WARFARE

Under Pachacuti and his successors, the Inca army was a formidable force, often numbering hundreds of thousands of soldiers. Every able-bodied man in the empire aged twenty-five to fifty was required to serve in the military whenever summoned. Thousands of miles of Inca roads ensured the ease of communications and troop movements. A network of storehouses full of food, clothing, and weapons guaranteed that Inca armies were always well supplied.

The citizen-soldiers of Tahuantinsuyu fought with a variety of weapons. For long-range fighting they used slings (which were often colorfully woven) to hurl egg-size stones at the enemy. Closer in they threw javelins, or they might throw weighted cords called bolas to entangle their foes' legs. For hand-to-hand combat they fought with a spiked mace on a rope or a warclub with a star-shaped head. These weapons could inflict severe head wounds—which Inca doctors often successfully treated by removing a portion of the skull to relieve pressure on the brain.

The Inca army's numbers and weapons were daunting enough. But to this they added a ferocity that is expressed in a popular battle song addressed to their enemies:

*We'll drink* chicha *from your skull*
*From your teeth we'll make a necklace*
*From your bones, flutes*
*From your skin we'll make a drum*
*And then we'll dance.**

No wonder, then, that many peoples were willing to accept Inca rule without a fight!

*quoted in *The Incredible Incas and Their Timeless Land* by Loren McIntyre, p.55

*Topa Yupanqui, shown here in a mid-eighteenth-century Peruvian painting, was renowned as a warrior. Under his command the Incas conquered most of western South America.*

## The Great Conquests

As Pachacuti grew older he spent his time in Cuzco, tending to government matters and supervising the complete rebuilding of the city. He turned over command of the armies to his son and heir, Topa (sometimes called Tupac) Yupanqui.

With victory after victory along the way, Topa led the Inca warriors as far north as Quito (KEE-toh), Ecuador. Then he turned back to the south, heading for the Peruvian coast. This region was desert, but many great cities had grown up where rivers cut across it on their way from the Andes to the Pacific. Topa subdued all of these cities, sometimes simply by cutting off their water supply. His greatest victory was over Chanchan, the capital of the extremely wealthy and powerful empire of Chimor ( CHEE-mor).

When Pachacuti died, in about 1471, Topa Yupanqui became Sapa Inca. He continued his wars of conquest, extending the empire's boundaries well into Bolivia and Argentina and all

*After Topa Yupanqui subdued Chimor, he had many Chimú nobles and artisans brought to Cuzco. Chimú ideas about administration may have influenced the way Topa organized and ran his empire. These drinking vessels, each made from a single sheet of silver, are good examples of the wealth and fine craftsmanship of the Chimú.*

the way south to the Maule River in what is now Chile. He also made forays into the rain forests of the lower eastern slopes of the Andes. By his death in around 1493, Tahuantinsuyu was nearly as large as it would ever be.

Topa Yupanqui was succeeded by his son Huayna (WY-nuh) Capac, who added more territory in the east and north. Like his father, he had especially great difficulty in the unfamiliar and uncomfortable environment of the eastern jungles. In the north, too, he and his army faced fierce resistance, and victories were hard-won. He set the empire's northern boundary at the Angasmayo (an-guhs-MY-oh) River, near the present border between Ecuador and Colombia.

Huayna Capac was responsible for bringing Ecuador fully into the life of the empire. In fact, he came to love this northern region with its lush greenery and mild climate. He spent most of his time in the Ecuadorian city of Tumebamba (too-meh-BAHM-buh), which he built up to such a splendor and importance that it rivaled Cuzco.

## The Beginning of the End

In Tumebamba in the year 1527, messengers brought Huayna Capac some unnerving news: Floating wooden houses had brought strange men with white skin and hair on their faces to Tumbes (TOOM-bez), on Peru's northern coast. The "bearded ones" were Spanish soldiers under the leadership of Francisco Pizarro. They soon sailed away, but the Sapa Inca had a foreboding that they would return and bring disaster to his people.

In fact, the Spaniards had already brought disaster to South America in the form of European diseases. The people of the western hemisphere had no immunity to these foreign illnesses, so their effect was devastating. In 1527 smallpox or measles swept through Tahuantinsuyu, killing an estimated 200,000 people. Among them were Huayna Capac, his sister-wife, and his heir.

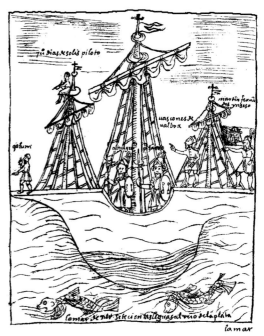

*Nothing in their experience prepared the Incas for the arrival of Pizarro and his soldiers. This picture of Pizarro's ship was drawn by a native artist after the conquest. Pizarro is the man with helmet and shield at the front of the ship, on the right.*

*Atahualpa, whose war with his brother devastated Tahuantinsuyu and made it vulnerable to the coming Spanish invasion*

In Cuzco, Huayna Capac's son Huascar (WAHS-kar) was chosen as Sapa Inca. But in Tumebamba another son, Atahualpa (a-tuh-WAHL-puh), was at the head of the great army that had made Huayna Capac's northern conquests. Before long the brothers had begun a civil war that would last for five years.

Both sides fought with merciless cruelty; hundreds of thousands of people were killed. Finally, in 1532, Atahualpa's forces captured Huascar, imprisoning him in the city of Xauxa (HOW-huh) in central Peru; he was later executed. The victorious army entered Cuzco, where they massacred Huascar's family and supporters.

Atahualpa himself had remained in the north during most of the fighting. Now he declared himself Sapa Inca and made his way to Cuzco to take control of Tahuantinsuyu. But during his journey he received momentous news: The bearded ones had returned.

## The Conquerors are Conquered

Atahualpa was curious about the strangers and sent an ambassador to invite them to visit him. Deceived by Spanish gifts and talk of peace, the ambassador returned to Atahualpa with the report that the bearded ones were not a threat. The Sapa Inca settled down in the royal palace outside the city of Cajamarca (kah-hah-MAR-kah), in northwestern Peru, to await his foreign visitors.

On November 15, 1532, Francisco Pizarro arrived in Cajamarca at the head of 106 foot soldiers, 62 horsemen, and an unknown number of native allies. The city had been evacuated at Atahualpa's order, but on the surrounding hillsides were camped tens of thousands of Inca warriors. Although the Spaniards were vastly outnumbered and deeply afraid, Pizarro sent a company of horsemen to meet Atahualpa and invite him into the city.

At dawn on the next day Pizarro prepared an ambush, stationing his men in the empty buildings around Cajamarca's main

# THE CONQUISTADORES

$S$ince Columbus's voyage to the West Indies in 1492, Spain had been steadily taking over land in the Americas. Thousands of Spaniards flocked to the new Spanish colonies to make their fortunes. One of these adventurers was Francisco Pizarro, an illiterate swineherd turned soldier. He fought in many battles in the Caribbean and Central America before settling in Panama around 1520.

But Pizarro was not content as a landowner. For some time the Spanish had been hearing rumors about a fabulously wealthy realm south of the equator. Then in 1521 Pizarro's relative Hernán Cortés conquered the Aztec Empire of Mexico; tales of the Aztecs' riches and Cortés's achievement soon reached Panama. Gradually Pizarro made up his mind to find and conquer the fabled golden land to the south.

Pizarro joined forces with the soldier Diego de Almagro and the priest Hernando Luque, who obtained funds for an expedition. In 1524 Pizarro and Almagro sailed south from Panama. They had no idea what the waters, lands, and peoples they would encounter were like—but they were convinced that wealth and glory were waiting for them. On this voyage, however, they did not even reach the northern boundary of Tahuantinsuyu, but were forced to turn back by a series of disasters.

Pizarro was undaunted. A man of immense courage and determination, he launched a second expedition in November 1526. This trip was even more difficult than the first one, but it was also more successful. Pizarro and his crew eventually reached the Inca town of Tumbes, where they were warmly welcomed. In Tumbes they saw many objects of gold and silver and a temple lavishly adorned with these metals, and they were told of the even greater splendors of Cuzco.

Now Pizarro knew he had found his land of gold. But he did not yet have the resources to conquer it. After his return to Panama, he set out for Spain. Charles V, king of Spain and Holy Roman Emperor, received him eagerly. The ruler was much interested in Pizarro's tales of his adventures and discoveries. He was also impressed by the beautifully woven cloth, gold and silver vases and ornaments, and llamas that Pizarro had brought along to prove the truth of his story.

Pizarro was given permission to raise troops for the conquest of Peru, and he was made governor and captain-general of the new colony. He also was firmly instructed to take Catholic priests with him to convert the natives to Christianity. Then Pizarro returned to Panama. In 1531, fired by the desire for gold and glory, Pizarro and his invasion force set out for the Inca empire, where they would soon become conquistadores (kahn-KEES-tuh-DOR-ays)—conquerors.

square. The Spaniards waited nervously all day for Atahualpa to arrive. Finally, at sunset, the Sapa Inca approached amid a splendid procession. Wearing a collar of emeralds and a tunic woven with gold threads, he rode in a litter carried by eighty bearers. Accompanying him were musicians, dancers, singers, and five thousand warriors—these, however, were dressed and armed for a ceremonial occasion, not for battle.

Atahualpa's procession crowded into the square. They were met by

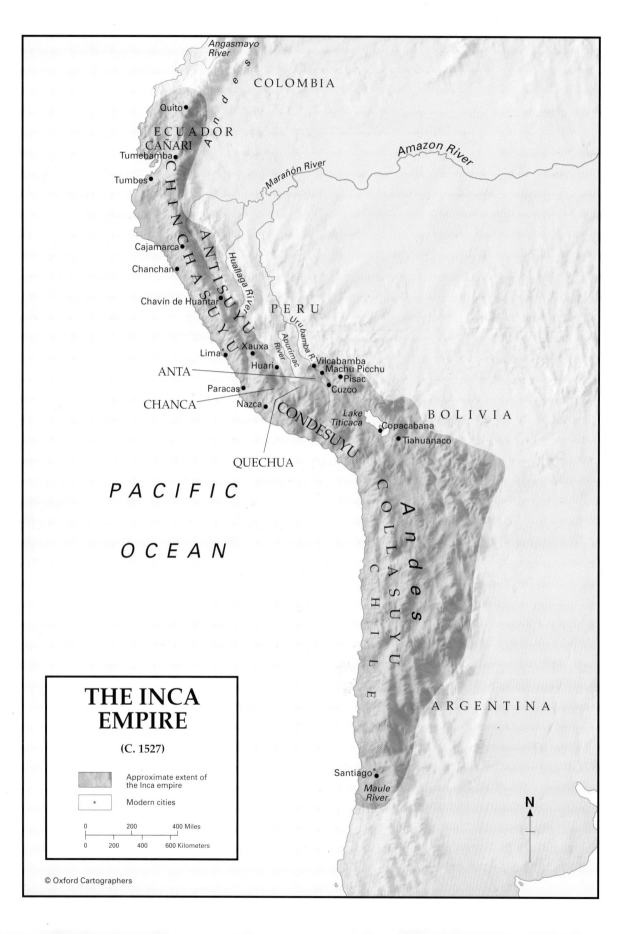

Angasmayo
River

COLOMBIA

Quito •

ECUADOR
CAÑARI
Tumebamba •

Amazon River

Tumbes •

Marañón River

C
H
I
N
C
H
A
S
U
Y
U

A
N
T
I
S
U
Y
U

Cajamarca •

Huallaga River

Chanchan •

Chavín de Huantar •

P E R U

Uru bamba River

Apurímac River

Lima •*   Xauxa •

Vilcabamba •
Machu Picchu •

ANTA

Huari •

Pisac •
Cuzco •

Paracas •

CHANCA

Nazca •

C
O
N
D
E
S
U
Y
U

Lake
Titicaca

BOLIVIA

QUECHUA

Copacabana •
• Tiahuanaco

PACIFIC

OCEAN

A
n
d
e
s

C
O
L
L
A
S
U
Y
U

C
H
I
L
E

ARGENTINA

THE INCA
EMPIRE

(C. 1527)

Approximate extent of
the Inca empire

*   Modern cities

0        200        400 Miles

0     200     400     600 Kilometers

Santiago •*

Maule
River

N

© Oxford Cartographers

a lone Spanish priest and a translator. The priest briefly explained the Christian faith to Atahualpa, urging him to convert. When the Sapa Inca showed no interest, the priest signaled to Pizarro to begin the attack.

Immediately the Spaniards fired a cannon into the crowd of Incas, and Pizarro's horsemen charged out of the buildings, swords and lances drawn. Many of Atahualpa's followers were trampled by the horses, and his lightly armed warriors were almost defenseless against the Euro-

*Pizarro and his men massacre Atahualpa's army in the main square of Cajamarca. This Spanish drawing portrays the Inca warriors according to European stereotypes of native peoples; in reality , the Incas would have been wearing clothes.*

pean weapons. Within half an hour it was all over. Thousands of Incas lay dead, and Atahualpa was Pizarro's prisoner. Eight months later the conquistadores executed Atahualpa for "crimes against the Spanish state."

In Tahuantinsuyu the Sapa Inca had held absolute authority. After Atahualpa's death, his people were almost completely without guidance and direction. In addition, they were still wrung out by the ravages of disease and civil war. Most did not have the heart to resist the Spanish invasion, even if they had wanted to. And then there were some who did not want to. Many people who had taken Huascar's side in the civil war, as well as tribes that had hated living under Inca rule, welcomed Pizarro and his men as liberators. The Spaniards were therefore able to recruit many allies within Tahuantinsuyu itself.

One year after Atahualpa's capture, the conquistadores marched into Cuzco almost unopposed. For the next three centuries the lands of Tahuantinsuyu would be Spanish colonies. But even time and foreign rule have not been able to completely erase the culture and achievements of the Incas.

# CHAPTER TWO

# GLORIES OF THE EMPIRE

The Incas always portrayed themselves as a people who brought civilization to a world full of savages. Official "rememberers" had the task of making sure that history celebrated the deeds of the Incas alone. The achievements of their forerunners and the people they conquered were purposefully forgotten.

In fact, Tahuantinsuyu was built on a foundation laid by many other cultures. The Incas were the inheritors of hundreds— even thousands—of years of developments in agriculture, arts and crafts, religion, and social organization. To this inheritance

*The ruins of the fortress of Sacsahuamán tower above visitors. The massive stone walls are enduring monuments to the accomplishments of the Incas.*

the Incas added their own prowess as conquerors and genius as organizers. The result was a civilization so accomplished that it has inspired awe in all who have studied it.

## Foundations of Greatness

The first important Andean civilization, called the Chavín (chah-VEEN) culture, had its beginnings around 800 B.C.E.* By this time agriculture had been well established in Peru for more than two thousand years. The Chavín people began the development of metalworking techniques and constructed impressive stone buildings.

The next great Peruvian civilizations flourished on the Pacific coast between roughly 200 B.C.E. and 600 C.E. In the north the Mochica (moh-CHEE-kuh) produced marvelous pottery jars and pitchers that realistically portrayed plants, animals, and people. Their neighbors in Paracas to the south wove and embroidered magnificent multicolored cloth. Still farther south, the people of Nazca crafted pottery almost as fine as that of the Mochica. They also made the mysterious Nazca Lines: abstract designs and pictures of animals, sometimes miles long, etched into the sand.

From about 600 to 1000 C.E. the central Andes were dominated by the cities of Huari (WAH-ree) in southern Peru and Tiahuanaco on the Bolivian side of Lake Titicaca. Huari seems to have been the capital of a militaristic empire. The Huari people built many cities and miles of roadways. Tiahuanaco was an important religious center. Its stone temples were already in ruins by the time the Sapa Inca Pachacuti saw them, but they were still impressive. The Incas believed that Tiahuanaco had been built by a race of giants or deities at the beginning of time.

The kingdom of Chimor, covering more than six hundred miles of the Peruvian coast, was the last major state to arise before the Incas. The capital, Chanchan, was a huge city with pyramids, temples, and houses of adobe brick. The Chimú had a

*Although they preserved little knowledge of their forerunners, the Incas had a rich heritage. The spirit of these ancient peoples lives on in their art, as in these clay jars. The man and the deer were crafted by Mochica potters, and the woman was made in Nazca.*

*Many systems of dating have been used by different cultures throughout history. This series of books uses B.C.E. (Before Common Era) and C.E. (Common Era) instead of B.C. (Before Christ) and A.D. (Anno Domini) out of respect for the diversity of the world's peoples.

well-developed messenger system and an extensive road network. They were masters of irrigation technology. Their goldsmiths and other artisans were extraordinarily skilled. After Topa Yupanqui conquered Chimor, he had many Chimú artisans brought to Cuzco to make fine objects for the Incas.

# A Civilization Without Writing

One of the great accomplishments of the Incas is that they were able to govern such a huge empire without having any system of writing. They did, however, have quipus (KEE-poos), record-keeping devices that had been used in Peru since pre-Inca times.

A quipu consisted of a main cord with colored strings of different lengths hanging from it. Knots were tied in these strings, which were arranged in groups. The knots represented numbers in a decimal counting system. For example, the number 2,304 would be recorded by two knots in the thousands position, three in the hundreds position, none in the tens position, and a four-looped knot in the ones position.

Every quipu was different and was meaningless without someone to interpret it. The makers, interpreters, and keepers of the quipus were called *quipucamayos* (KEE-poo-kah-MY-ohs). These men were specially trained from childhood. They were sent to all parts of the empire and made regular reports to the government. The *quipucamayos* kept records of such things as population, number of troops, size of animal herds, crop yields, inventory of storehouses, and amounts of tribute.

## Literature Without Books

According to some sources, quipus were also used as an aid to memorizing and recalling history, mythology, poetry, and stories. Probably the *quipucamayos* did have the responsibility of passing on the Incas' oral literature. This responsibility was shared by the *amautas* (ah-MOW-tahs), "wise men," who created many of the stories.

The *amautas* also composed plays that were performed at the Sapa Inca's court. There were dramas about wars, heroes, and the great deeds of past rulers, and comedies about family life, agriculture, and the like. The music of drums and flutes accompanied these plays, which were acted by members of the nobility.

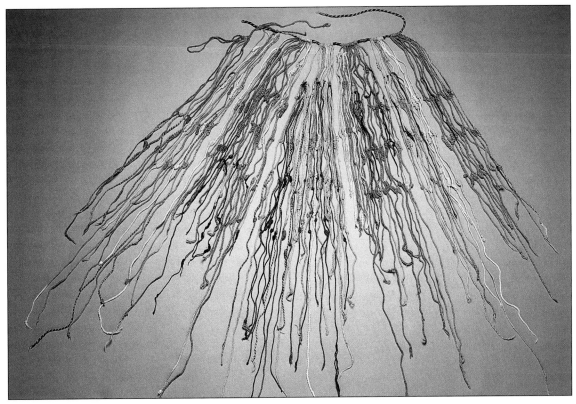

A quipu. *Unfortunately, there is no way for anyone now to tell what the knots on these strings record.*

Love poems and songs were popular with all social classes. Other types of poetry included prayers, hymns, and laments for the dead. Narrative poems and songs—those that told a story—had an especially important place in Inca culture. Chiefs and heads of families preserved the history of their ancestors in such works. At public ceremonies, narratives were sung or recited to celebrate the deeds of the Sapa Inca and his forebears.

## An Empire Rooted in Farming

The Incas had a thorough understanding of agriculture and extremely efficient farming methods. They spread these methods to all the lands they conquered. Most harvests produced huge surpluses of food, which were stored in warehouses throughout the empire. Without such a reliable food supply, many of the Incas' other achievements would have been impossible.

*Many terraced fields have been in continuous use by Andean farmers since the days of the Incas. These terraces are in the Pisac valley, near Cuzco.*

To grow enough crops, the people of the Andes had to create farmland on the mountainsides. They did this by constructing terraces. To make a terrace, a stone wall eight to fourteen feet high was built. The area behind this retaining wall was filled with soil, which workers carried up from the river valleys. The finished terrace would be three to fifteen feet wide, depending on the steepness of the slope it was built on. There might be as many as a hundred terraces, one above the other, on a single hillside. An efficient irrigation system assured that each of these fields received enough water.

## The Basics of Life

The Incas' staple crops were potatoes, maize (corn), and quinoa (KEEN-wah). Potatoes were so basic to the Incas' culture that they measured time in units equal to how long it took to boil a potato. More than two hundred varieties of potato were cultivated in Tahuantinsuyu. Potatoes could grow at altitudes up to three miles above sea level and they could withstand frost. They were often used to make *chuño* (CHOO-nyoh), freeze-dried potatoes that could be stored for long periods.

Dried maize could be stored for even longer, but the plants had to be grown at lower elevations where frost would not kill them. The Incas cultivated many different types of maize. It was eaten toasted hard or boiled soft. For special occasions it was ground into flour that was used for cakes, porridge, or dumplings. Popcorn was sometimes made as a treat. The favorite drink of the Incas, *chicha* (CHEE-chah), was brewed from fermented maize.

Quinoa is a plant whose tasty grainlike seeds are rich in protein. These seeds were eaten in soups and stews. The leaves were cooked and eaten much like spinach. Quinoa flourished on high mountain slopes.

The Incas also grew many kinds of root crops, including sweet potatoes. In warmer valleys chili peppers and squash were cultivated. From the hot lowlands came tomatoes, avocados, several kinds of beans, peanuts, bananas, guavas, and other produce.

## THE INCAS' SACRED PLANT

A major nonfood crop was coca, raised on plantations at the edge of the jungle in Tahuantinsuyu's eastern quarter. Coca leaves played an important role in Inca religion. They were scattered or burned as offerings. In rituals and at festivals people chewed them to help produce a state of ecstasy. Chewing coca leaves released small doses of the stimulant cocaine, which also helped relieve hunger and fatigue. For this reason coca was sometimes provided for people engaged in especially hard work. Otherwise it was regarded as a luxury, one of the privileges of the elite; noblemen had beautifully woven shoulder bags just for carrying coca leaves. Habitual use was frowned on, however, and the distribution of coca was strictly controlled by the Inca government.

### Useful Animals

The Incas' main source of meat was the guinea pig. Most families kept guinea pigs in their houses. The little animals ran about tamely, eating food scraps, until they were wanted. Then they were roasted over an open fire or boiled in a stew.

The most important domestic animals were llamas and alpacas. These had been raised in the high plateaus of Bolivia and

*Llamas are still used as beasts of burden in the Andes.*

southern Peru for more than two thousand years before the rise of Tahuantinsuyu. The Incas had huge herds throughout the empire.

The two animals were bred for different purposes, but both provided manure that was used as fertilizer and also as fuel. Both were sacrificed in important religious rituals. Occasionally they were slaughtered for meat and leather. When the meat was dried in thin strips, it was called *charqui* (CHAR-kee)—the source of our word *jerky.* The animals' bones were used for making a wide range of objects, including needles, flutes, and beads.

Llamas were employed as pack animals; they could carry up to a hundred pounds six to twelve miles a day. Their coarse hair was used to make sacks, ropes, halters, and heavy blankets. Alpacas were raised for their soft wool, which was made into clothing.

The finest wool came from a wild relative of the llama and alpaca. This small, shy creature was the vicuña (vi-KOO-nyuh). Every year the Sapa Inca led a great royal hunt in which thousands of animals were rounded up. The vicuñas were sheared and set free, and their wool was saved to be made into garments for the ruler and those he specially favored.

## Cloth: More Precious than Gold

By 100 B.C.E. the people of Paracas on Peru's southern coast had mastered every known weaving technique. They produced what has been called the most elaborate and exquisite handwoven cloth ever made anywhere in the world. The Incas therefore had a very long tradition of superb weaving to draw on. They also had a keen appreciation for the hundreds or even thousands of hours that went into producing a single piece of cloth. Their finest textiles were more valuable to them than gold.

Weaving was usually done on a backstrap loom. One end of this loom was fastened to a post, peg, or tree, and a belt at the other end wrapped around the waist of the weaver, who sat on the ground. The weaver leaned backward or forward to control the tension of the warp (long) threads. For wide cloth, an upright loom propped against a wall was used. Weaving was generally done by women, but heavy cloth was often made by men. Men were also responsible for making sandals, which were worn by both sexes and all social classes.

### Homespun and Splendor

The common people made their own clothing. For most garments they wove cloth with simple stripes or geometric patterns in the natural whites, grays, and browns of alpaca wool. On the hot Pacific coast, people made their clothing out of cotton, which grew in six different colors.

The clothing of the nobles, on the other hand, was woven from brilliantly dyed fibers, often in extremely complex designs. The most elaborate cloth of all was called *cumbi* (KUM-bee) and was made of vicuña wool. The Sapa Inca sometimes gave this cloth to people he wanted to specially favor or reward; otherwise *cumbi* garments could be worn only by the royal family.

Royalty and nobles had other types of splendid clothing as well. Copper, silver, or gold ornaments might be sewn all over a garment, or

*Men's tunics from Inca-ruled coastal Peru. One is woven of undyed cotton, while the other—clearly a nobleman's garment—is made of alpaca wool covered with small gold plaques.*

golden threads might be woven right into the cloth. Some clothing was covered with designs made of brightly colored feathers, which were brought from the rain forests in great quantities. The Sapa Inca even had clothes woven from rare, silklike bat wool.

## Simple Styles

Whether for nobles or commoners, clothing was simply made: A rectangular piece of cloth was folded in half and a slit was cut in the center for the wearer's head. Men wore a sort of knee-length poncho, sewn up the sides under the arms. Over this they knotted a short mantle, or cape. Nobles and warriors sometimes wore fringes around their knees and ankles. In addition, men of the highest classes had their ears pierced for large ear spools, which were made of precious metals or of wood inlaid with shells or feathers.

Women dressed in a sleeveless ankle-length garment that was open on the sides. It was held in place by a very wide woven belt. Over their shoulders they draped a mantle, which was fastened with a copper, bronze, silver, or gold pin called a *tupu* (TU-poo). The heads of *tupus* were generally large, flat, oval or half-moon shaped, with edges sharp enough to cut the thread that Inca women spent so much time spinning and weaving.

## Masters of Metalwork

Like weaving, metalworking had a long history in South America. From the time of the ancient Chavín culture, metals had been much used for jewelry and religious objects. The most accomplished metalworkers in the Americas before the Spanish arrived were the Chimú and the Incas.

By 700 C.E. bronze, a blend of copper and tin, had come into use in South America. Bronze was strong and versatile; it was especially suitable for making tools. Yet it was not widely utilized for several hundred years—not until the Incas recognized its virtues and spread its use throughout their empire. Inca metalworkers crafted all sorts of objects from bronze, including tweezers, mirrors, needles, bells, ax blades, warclub heads, chisels, crowbars, and knives.

## Land of Gold

Although bronze working was one of Tahuantinsuyu's greatest contributions to South American culture, the Incas have always been best known for their incredible wealth of gold. Many of the Inca conquests were probably made in order to acquire more mines. However, the Incas placed no monetary value on gold—indeed, they had no form of money at all.

*This beautiful 9.5-inch model of an alpaca is one of the very few silver or gold objects to survive the Spanish conquest of Tahuantinsuyu.*

The Incas valued precious metals and gems for their beauty and for their symbolism. They called gold "the sweat of the Sun" and associated it with the sun god and his representative on earth, the Sapa Inca. Silver was "the tears of the Moon"; it was especially identified with the queen. Numerous gold- and silver-smiths lived in Cuzco, crafting exquisite objects for the sole use of royalty and religious institutions.

The Sapa Inca was surrounded by vast amounts of gold, silver, and gems. The litters in which he traveled and the stools on which he sat were covered or inlaid with these precious materials. His plates, water jars, and other everyday objects were made of gold and silver. He awarded golden cups to nobles whom he wanted to honor. In his palace garden, gold and silver flowers and maize "grew" alongside the actual plants, and a wide variety of gold and silver animals were realistically posed among them.

There was a similarly splendid garden in a courtyard of the main temple in Cuzco. Along with golden maize plants, there were golden clods of dirt, golden tufts of grass, and a life-size herd of twenty golden llamas with their golden shepherds. The temple walls were covered with plates of gold, and golden threads were woven into the thatched roof. No wonder that the temple was called Coricancha (koh-ree-KAHN-chah), "the Golden Enclosure."

*This pottery figure carries an* aryballus *jar on his back.*

While the Sapa Inca and his favored nobles used cups and dishes made of precious metals, for most people of Tahuantinsuyu these items were made of clay. Inca pottery was almost as hard as metal and was finished with a smooth, polished surface. Jars, cups, and plates were usually decorated with brightly colored geometric designs. Plates were made with handles, which might be modeled in the shape of bird, human, or puma heads. One of the most typical forms of Inca pottery was the *aryballus* jar, which could be as large as a person. It had a narrow neck, pointed bottom, and a pair of low handles for a strap to go through so that it could be hung up or carried. The Incas also made their cooking pots and even their stoves out of clay.

Although wood was rare in many parts of the Andes, it was a favorite material for cups. Wide-mouthed wooden cups, which could hold one to two quarts of *chicha,* were called *keros* (KEH-rohs). They were decorated with carved geometric patterns, designs in colored lacquer, or inlays of lead. *Keros* played an important role in Inca life: They were used especially for entertaining guests and for making ceremonial toasts. They were made by professional woodworkers called *kero-camayohs,* or "cup specialists."

## Cities of Stone

At the time of the Chanca war, the buildings of Cuzco were constructed of sod, adobe, and fieldstone. Most were probably small, with only one room, and they were clustered together haphazardly. But after Pachacuti became Sapa Inca, he set about completely rebuilding the city. He drew his inspirations from the layouts of the Huari cities and the monumental stonework of Tiahuanaco.

Central Cuzco was given roughly the shape of a crouching puma (mountain lion), a symbol of strength and power. Only royalty, the very highest nobility, and those who served in the temples were allowed to live in this area. At the puma's head the great fortress of Sacsahuamán (sahk-sah-wah-MAHN) was erected. Coricancha was at the puma's hindquarters; Pachacuti personally marked out the temple's outlines before it was built. Between the puma's front and back legs was the main square, called

# ROADS TO POWER

The Inca empire was bound together by more than ten thousand miles of roadway. There were two main roads, which ran parallel to each other: one through the highlands and one through the coastal desert. These were linked by numerous roads running between them, and roads also ran from the highland route into the eastern jungles.

When the Spaniards arrived in Tahuantinsuyu, they marveled at the Inca road system, which was superior to any they had ever seen. The roads were fifteen to twenty-four feet wide. Near cities they were paved with stone. When they passed through farmland, they had walls on each side to keep travelers from disturbing the crops. Causeways were built to carry the roads over swampy ground. If the roadway had to climb a steep mountain, steps were cut into the rock itself. For crossing rivers, various kinds of bridges were constructed, including rope suspension bridges that swayed high above river gorges.

The main purpose of these roads was military; they assured that Inca armies could get to wherever they were needed as quickly as possible—whether to head out on new conquests or to put down rebellions in already-conquered territories. But roads were also used by the llama caravans that took goods from one part of the empire to another. And the roadways were essential for keeping the provinces in communication with the capital.

Every one or two miles along the roads were little huts where runners called *chasquis* were stationed. Each *chasqui* had an assigned stretch of roadway, which he knew so well that he could run it on a moonless night. When a *chasqui* was given a message he ran as fast as he could to the next post, blowing a conch-shell trumpet to announce his approach. The next chasqui would be waiting for him and would set off at top speed as soon as the message had been passed along. In this way news, orders, and official business traveled through the empire at the rate of around two hundred miles a day. It is said that *chasquis* were also used to bring the Sapa Inca fresh fish from the coast for his dinner.

Travelers on an Inca road never had to worry about what to eat or where to spend the night. All along the road, about twelve miles apart, were way stations called *tampus*. These provided places to sleep and were well stocked with food, blankets, and other supplies. The *tampus* were maintained by the people of the surrounding area—most of whom probably never traveled on the road themselves. Only people engaged on the empire's business were allowed to use the Incas' roads.

A chasqui, *portrayed by the native artist Huaman Poma, blows his conch-shell trumpet.*

Huacapata (WAH-kah-PAH-tah), "the Holy Plaza," where daily rituals and splendid seasonal ceremonies were held. From Huacapata four roads extended, running to each of the four quarters of the empire.

## Monumental Accomplishments

The palaces and temples of Pachacuti's Cuzco—and of all the Inca cities from then on—were huge structures built of massive stones.

*Cuzco's best-preserved Inca wall. Just to the right of the woman (who is spinning with a drop spindle) is the stone with twelve corners.*

No mortar of any kind was used to hold these blocks in place. It wasn't needed—stones were so carefully cut and fitted together that even today a knife blade cannot be inserted between them.

For some walls, rectangular stones of roughly the same size were laid in even rows, like brickwork. Other walls were made of blocks of all different shapes and sizes, fitted together like pieces in a jigsaw puzzle. One famous stone in the wall of a palace, which can be seen today, has twelve corners on its outward side alone; it interlocks perfectly with the stones around it.

The construction of such buildings was an amazing feat. Some of the stones in Cuzco's buildings came from as far as twenty-one miles away. And the stones were gigantic—in the foundation of Sacsahuamán, for example, are blocks weighing as much as 126 tons. Thousands of men had to haul these stones using nothing more than wooden rollers and great leather or plant-fiber ropes. Some stones never made it to their destination—it was said that the stones were too tired to go on, and so they were left lying along the roadside.

At the construction site, the stones were hauled up earthen ramps and then moved into position with the help of bronze crowbars. Before their final placement, they had to be shaped to fit with the surrounding blocks. The Incas had no iron tools to assist with this task; they pounded the blocks into shape using hard river stones—and a lot of strength and patience.

The efforts of the Inca architects and stoneworkers paid off. Despite the ravages of conquest, earthquake, and time, a great many of the Incas' wonderfully constructed buildings still stand, bearing witness to an empire of unforgettable greatness.

# CHAPTER THREE

# DIVINE POWERS

The Incas' religion was a practical one. It was mainly concerned with the forces of nature on which life depended. The Inca rulers also made practical use of their religion as a means of unifying the many peoples of Tahuantinsuyu. This policy began with Pachacuti, the first great Inca conqueror. He was also responsible for giving Inca mythology and worship standard forms. Nevertheless, many other beliefs continued to exist side by side with those promoted by Pachacuti.

*The figure depicted on this silver pendant from Chimor may represent one of the gods worshiped in Peru during Inca times.*

## The Creation

*At the beginning of time, the god Viracocha created the world. At first it was all darkness, but then Viracocha created the Sun, the Moon, and the Stars. He created the Thunder, the Earth, and the Sea. Finally he took stone and out of it made human beings. Then Viracocha walked among the people, showing them how to live. When he reached the coast, he went away over the sea—but someday he would return.*

This is one of the many creation myths that were told in Tahuantinsuyu. In a variation, it was said that Viracocha gave birth to the Sun and Moon, who in turn were the parents of the Morning Star and the Evening Star. The Morning Star became the father of Lord Earth, the ancestor of men. The Evening Star was the mother of Lady Ocean, the ancestor of women.

After the creation, according to other myths, a great flood came and covered even the highest mountain peaks. All the people were killed in the flood, so when it was over Viracocha made new people out of clay. On them he painted clothes and hair in the styles that should be worn by each nation. He gave each

*The creator god Viracocha is featured at the center of this feathered neckpiece.*

nation of people its own language and songs, as well as seeds for the food plants they should grow. Then Viracocha sent the people beneath the earth, telling them where they should come out and settle. Some nations emerged from caves or hills, some from tree trunks, some from springs and lakes. After the people made of clay had children, they turned into birds and animals, who were worshiped by their descendants.

Some sources say that Viracocha was not the creator of the world, but that he did cause the sun to shine, and he taught people how to live. Still other myths describe Viracocha as the creator only of the first Incas, whom he sent to civilize the people already living on the earth. For the most part, however, the Incas seem to have regarded Viracocha as the ultimate source of everything that existed in their world. He was often described as an invisible, behind-the-scenes power. All of the other deities received their authority from him.

## Deities of Sky, Water, and Earth

The god most worshiped by the Incas was Inti (IN-tee), the Sun. He was called the Giver of Life. It is easy to see why, since the Andean heights were almost unbearably cold unless the sun was shining. And without the sun's light and warmth, no crops would grow to feed the people.

Sun worship was the official religion of the Inca empire. The rulers regarded the Sun as their ancestor and called themselves the Sons of the Sun. They had temples dedicated to Inti built in all the lands they conquered.

The main temple in Cuzco, Coricancha, had the empire's most splendid Sun shrine. On the wall was a huge image of the Sun, depicted as a man's face surrounded by rays, made of a sheet of gold and decorated with jewels. It was hung facing east so that the rays of the rising sun would reflect off it and make it shine. Around this image were magnificently dressed statues of past Inca rulers seated on golden thrones. A band of gold eleven inches wide was set into the walls all the way around the shrine.

### The Weather God

After Viracocha and Inti, the most important god was Illapa (ee-YAH-pah), the Thunder. He was described as the messenger and servant of the Sun. People prayed to him for rain. He had a shrine in Coricancha.

*A participant in a modern-day festival near Cuzco plays the role of Inti, the Sun, very much as Inca priests did in the temples of Tahuantinsuyu hundreds of years ago.*

The Incas thought of Illapa as a man who was made of stars and lived in the sky. He carried a war club in one hand and a sling in the other. His garments shone, giving off lightning flashes when he hurled a stone from his sling. The crack of the sling in the air was the sound of thunder. The stone broke a water jar that his sister had filled at a river in the sky—the Milky Way. From the jar rain poured out to water the crops.

### Divine Mothers

The Incas had several important goddesses. Mama-Quilla (MAH-mah-KEE-yah), the Moon, was the wife of Inti. Temples were built to her all over the empire. The walls of her shrine at Coricancha were covered with sheets of silver, and on one wall hung a large silver image of the moon with a woman's face. Statues of past Inca queens, Mama-Quilla's representatives on earth, were arranged around this image.

The goddess of water was Mama-cocha (MAH-mah-KOH-chah). On the coast she was identified with the ocean, and the people there prayed to her for calm seas and good fishing. In the mountains Mama-cocha was associated with lakes and rivers.

The most worshiped goddess was probably Pacha-mama (PAH-chah-MAH-mah), Mother Earth. Her symbol was a long stone that was placed in the middle of a field. People came to such stones to pray to Pacha-mama, asking her to protect the fields and make them fertile. An earth god named Pachacamac (PAH-chah-KAH-mahk) was sometimes said to be her husband.

There were several other goddesses related to agriculture. For example Mamazara (MAH-mah-ZAH-rah), Mother Maize, assured the production and preservation of the grain. Every year after the harvest each farmer saved a bit of maize, wrapped up in some of the family's best cloth, in a storage bin. This bin was then called Mamazara and was a focus of worship throughout the year.

---

### AN INCA PRAYER TO THE SUN

"O Sun, my father, who said 'Let there be Cuzco!' and by your will it was founded and it is preserved with such grandeur! Let these sons of yours, the Incas, be conquerors and despoilers of all mankind. . . . Let them be prosperous and make them happy, and do not allow them to be conquered by anyone, but let them always be conquerors, since you made them for that purpose."

—recorded by
Father Bernabe Cobo before 1653
(translated by Roland Hamilton)

## THE SUN AND MOON AT COPACABANA

Not far out from Lake Titicaca's southern shore, near the town of Copacabana, were two islands dedicated to the Sun and the Moon. On the Island of Titicaca there had been a temple to the Sun even before Inca rule came to the area. The emperor Topa Yupanqui decided to enlarge this temple and devote the whole town of Copacabana to the Sun's worship. And since the Moon was the wife of the Sun, Topa had a temple to the Moon built on the nearby island of Coati (koh-AH-tee).

The priests of Titicaca and the priestesses of Coati communicated with each other frequently, traveling between the islands on rafts. The priestesses would take the part of the Moon and send the Sun loving messages, which the priests, taking the Sun's part, would answer with great tenderness. Sometimes, in a kind of religious drama, a priest and priestess were chosen to represent the Sun and the Moon. They would meet at one of the temples and toast each other with *chicha*. Then the "Moon" would caress the "Sun" and beg him to shine constantly on the fields until it came time for the rains. The "Sun" would graciously agree to send his warmth and light to the growing crops—just as the people of Tahuantinsuyu prayed the real Sun would do.

*Lake Titicaca, one of the holiest places in the Inca empire*

### Heavenly Guardians

The Incas called the stars the children of the Sun and the Moon. They believed that every species of animal and bird had a particular star or constellation as its divine guardian. For example the constellation Uruchillay (oo-roo-CHEE-yi), which we know as Lira, was imagined as a large two-colored llama. Llama herders therefore worshiped Uruchillay, who cared for the livestock. A star called Machacuay (mah-chah-KOO-i) watched over snakes, so people prayed to it for protection from snake bites. People turned to Chuquichinchay (choo-kee-CHIN-chi), a star regarded as a jaguar, for protection against jaguars, bears, and pumas.

Everyone worshiped the star cluster that we call the Pleiades (PLEE-uh-deez); the Inca name for it was Collca (KOY-kah), which means "storehouse." According to one source, Collca was responsible for the preservation of seed. Another source states that all of the other stars, along with the power to conserve the birds and animals, came from Collca. For this reason the Incas often gave it the honored title *Mama.*

## Holy People, Places, and Things

In the Inca world, divine power was not limited to the deities. A magical and spiritual force was believed to exist in any special or unusual person, place, or object. Whatever possessed this force was called a *huaca* (WAH-kah) and was worshiped much as the gods and goddesses were.

People might be *huacas* if they were born with a birthmark or if there was something unusual about their birth. Twins and triplets, therefore, were considered *huacas.* They were treated with great respect and were required to do only light work, or none at all.

Many kinds of places were *huacas.* Some of the most holy were the caves and other locations that

the earliest people were said to have emerged from. Also regarded as especially sacred were mountains; the taller they were, the more powerful. Many features of the landscape—such as springs, cliffs, gorges, and exceptionally large trees—were worshiped as *huacas*. Battlefields, meeting places, and other sites connected with past Inca rulers were also considered *huacas*. Temples and tombs were

*Snow-covered mountains, as sources of water but also of blizzards and avalanches, were especially powerful* huacas.

*huacas,* and so were stones that were set up to mark the sun's position at certain important points of the year.

Any stone that was unusual—in size, shape, position, location—could be a *huaca.* Other objects that were considered *huacas* included precious metals (along with the mines they came from) and oddly shaped vegetables. Statues of deities or other images of divine forces were important *huacas.* For protection, people carried with them small figures of humans, plants, or animals, and these were called *huacas,* too.

## The Honored Dead

Like many peoples, the Incas worshiped their ancestors. The bodies of the dead were often preserved as mummies, a practice with a long history in the dry climate of the Andes and the coastal desert. Sometimes the mummies were buried with many of their possessions. Otherwise they were kept in the homes of their descendants, where they were given regular offerings of food and drink.

The mummies of former rulers received very special treatment, according to the decree of Pachacuti. Each one had its own palace in Cuzco, full of all the precious objects that the ruler had collected during his life. The ruler's remains were cared for by a group of his descendants called a *panaca* (pah-NAH-kah). The members of the *panaca* attended the mummy just as they would have attended a living ruler: They prepared fine food and *chicha* for it, adorned it with elaborate textiles and golden ornaments, shooed flies away from it, and entertained it. People came to worship the mummy and consult it on important matters; a man and a woman of the *panaca* gave advice on the mummy's behalf.

The dead rulers were carried about Cuzco on litters, visiting one another as well as calling on the living. On the most important festivals the royal mummies were brought out to the city's main square in great splendor. There they toasted one another (through their attendants) with gold and silver tumblers full of *chicha.*

## Rituals of Devotion

In the Andes, with their harsh environment and majestic scenery, people were constantly aware of powers greater than themselves. The favor and

## THE INCAS' AFTERLIFE

The souls of dead Inca rulers were believed to live forever with the Sun, where they enjoyed luxury and plenty. From this exalted place they were able to help and protect those who prayed to them. Nobles and virtuous commoners also went to live with the Sun after death. But commoners who had done evil or had broken the law spent the afterlife in a dark, cramped place underground, where they always suffered from hunger and thirst.

protection of these divine powers were crucial to everything from farming to travel to war. Worship and prayer were therefore a part of everyday life for the people of Tahuantinsuyu. They had many ways of showing their devotion to their deities, *huacas,* and dead.

One form of reverence before a temple, *huaca,* mummy, or statue of a deity was called *mocha.* Worshipers bowed from the waist, with their heads as low as possible and their arms stretched out in front of them, and made a kissing sound, then kissed their fingertips. This gesture was also performed before the Sapa Inca and the nobles.

When people drank *chicha,* they dipped their fingers into the liquid and then sprinkled it toward the sun, the earth, or the fire. As they did so they prayed for life and contentment. When walking by a river, people made a point of taking a drink from it as a sign of respect. If they passed a *huaca,* they would throw to it chewed coca leaves, feathers, maize, or even a couple of their eyelashes or eyebrow hairs. They then asked the *huaca* to let them travel in peace and to give them the strength to finish their journey successfully.

Prayers could be made silently or aloud. Some were improvised and some were set prayers that had been handed down for generations. Many of these had been composed by Pachacuti.

### Confession

People went to the *huacas* to confess their sins. The priest or priestess of the *huaca* would listen to the confession and use divination to decide whether the confession was entirely truthful. If it wasn't, the priest or priestess hit the person on the back with a stone several times and then made him or her confess again. When the confession was complete and acceptable, the person went to wash in a river, sending the sins away down the river and into the sea. To atone for the sins, the person could not eat salt or chili pepper for a certain number of days, and might also have to abstain from meat.

Confessions were usually made if there was illness in the family, since diseases were believed to be caused by sinful behavior. The greatest sin was disobeying the laws and commands of the Sapa Inca. If the Sapa Inca was ill, it was because of the sins of his subjects, and so they all went to confession. (The Sapa Inca himself confessed directly to the Sun.) Confessions were also routinely made before a sacrifice.

## Sacrifice

The Incas believed that sacrifices were necessary for life to continue and for the empire to prosper. Sacrifices might take the form of simple or elaborate offerings. At plowing, sowing, and harvesting, coca leaves were scattered over the ground and *chicha* was poured out for Pacha-Mama, the Earth. Seashells were offered at springs and streams, the daughters of the sea, to thank them for irrigating the fields and to keep them doing so. Gold and silver nuggets or objects were sacrificed at various *huacas* either by being buried or by being hung on temple walls.

As in many cultures of the past, domestic animals were often sacrificed. Guinea pigs were frequently used, but the animals for major sacrifices were llamas or alpacas. Sometimes the animals were burned, usually with other items, in specially built fires. In Cuzco's main plaza every morning at sunrise, a white llama, baskets of coca leaves, and food were sacrificed to the Sun in this way. More sacrifices were made to the Sun on the first day of each month. Their purpose was to thank the Sun for his light and his help in growing crops, and to give him the strength to continue to do these things. Similarly, sacrifices of two-colored llamas were made to the Thunder so that he would always provide enough rain for the crops.

On extremely important occasions or in times of great distress, children and adolescents were sacrificed. Every year in each of the major temples a male infant and a female infant were sacrificed. This sacrifice

*This elaborate ceremonial knife, called a* tumi, *may have been used in important sacrifice rituals.*

was also made if there was a war, a serious food shortage, a major out-break of disease, a natural disaster, or if the Sapa Inca was ill.

The most important occasion in Tahuantinsuyu was the coronation of a new Sapa Inca. It was crucial to do everything possible to guarantee him a long reign, good health, many sons, victory in war, peace among his subjects, and an abundant food supply for the empire. Two hundred young people were ritually killed, then specially buried with objects of gold and silver.

Many of these children were taken from their parents as a form of tax, but sometimes parents voluntarily gave their children for sacrifice. The boys were usually about ten years old; girls were between ten and sixteen. Both had to be physically perfect, with no blemishes of any kind. The Incas were always careful to give their deities the best of everything they had.

Opposite: *This small gold statue, wrapped in a beautiful mantle pinned with a miniature gold* tupu, *is similar to figures that archaeologists recently found beside the body of a young woman who was sacrificed at the summit of a mountain in southern Peru. The young woman was also dressed in finely woven garments and she wore an elaborate feather headdress.*

# CHAPTER FOUR

# LIFE UNDER THE SON OF THE SUN

At its height, Tahuantinsuyu had a population of roughly seven million people, who came from as many as one hundred different tribes or nations. This vast and diverse empire was held together by one force: the authority of the Sapa Inca. The emperor was regarded as the Son of the Sun, and so as the Sun's earthly representative. He therefore ruled by divine right and was nearly a god himself. It was said that just as the rays of the Sun reached to every part of the world, so the power of the Son of the Sun reached to every part of the empire.

*With its red fringe, this indicates a Sapa Inca's headdress. At one time there may also have been a gold plume above the fringe.*

## An Absolute Ruler

The Sapa Inca was the head of the government, the military, and the state religion. His power was absolute, checked only by custom and the need to keep his subjects contented enough not to rebel. In theory, all the men of the empire were his sons, and all the women were his wives. The Sapa Inca also claimed the ownership of all farmland, llama and alpaca herds, game animals, mines, and precious metals. Although this may not have been entirely true in practice, it is certain that the Sapa Inca controlled most of the resources of his realm, either directly or indirectly.

As the Son of the Sun, the emperor was set apart from his subjects by many customs

Guaina Capac Duodesimo. Ynqa,

and privileges. He wore a unique headdress with a fringe of red vicuña-wool tassels across his forehead—this was his crown. When he went out, he rode in a splendid litter, preceded by runners who announced his coming. He usually ate alone, waited on by his concubines, or secondary wives; only a few of

*The Sapa Inca Huayna Capac, portrayed by an eighteenth-century Peruvian artist, wears sun faces on his tunic and headdress to declare the divine source of his power.*

**47**

his sons were privileged enough to occasionally dine with him. Visitors to his court had to show their respect by removing their sandals and wearing token burdens on their backs. They may not even have been permitted to look at the Sapa Inca, who often sat behind a screen.

## The Empress

In a tradition begun by Pachacuti, when a new emperor was crowned he married one of his full sisters. This sister-wife was called the Coya (a title that had been used for Inca queens before the time of Pachacuti as well). As the Sapa Inca's full sister, the Coya was also a descendant of the Sun. So although the ruler might have hundreds of other wives, only one of the Coya's sons could be chosen as the heir to the throne. This guaranteed that the royal and divine heritage of the Sun would be passed on to the next emperor.

The Coya was highly respected. She was identified with the Moon and the Earth and played an important role in many rituals, especially those concerned with agriculture. She might take a behind-the-scenes role in government. Her ideal qualities were religious devotion, gentleness, charm, understanding, prudence, and beauty. The people of Tahuantinsuyu affectionately called her Mamanchic, "Our Mother." Many Coyas were noted for their kindness to the elderly and the poor.

The Coya kept a garden that was praised for the variety of flowers, food plants, and animals in it. One Coya, Chimbo Urma Mama Yachi, the wife of the fourth ruler, was credited with introducing many new plants to be farmed. It was said that she also encouraged fishing and experimented with using snake venom to poison arrowheads. Ipahuaco (ee-pah-WAH-koh) Mama Machi Coya, the wife of Yahuar Huaca, was especially remembered for breeding and domesticating monkeys, parrots, macaws, and small birds.

Like her husband, the Coya enjoyed great wealth and special

### THE EMPEROR'S NEW CLOTHES

The later Inca emperors were so exalted—and so wealthy—that they wore their splendid garments only once. Every evening the Sapa Inca's clothes were gathered up and stored. Every morning he put on a brand-new outfit. At the end of the year, with great ceremony, all of the once-worn clothes were burned.

treatment. She had her own palace, where she was attended by the *ñustas* (NYOOS-tahs), or royal maidens. She spent much time socializing and hosting entertainments, although she ate alone. She bathed and changed her clothes twice a day. When she went out walking, servants held a canopy of colorful feathers and silver bells over her head, while others laid cloths in front of her so that she would not have to step on the bare ground.

## Incas and Adopted Incas

Although today we often use the word *Incas* to refer to all the people of the Inca empire, this name had a much more specific meaning in Tahuantinsuyu. Only men who could claim to be descended from Manco Capac, the legendary first ruler of Cuzco, could be called Incas. (Women of royal descent were called *ñustas* before they married and *pallas* [PAH-yahs] afterward.) Also known as Capac Incas, these men were the highest nobility of the realm and were entrusted with all government, religious, and military posts.

As the empire rapidly expanded under Pachacuti, however, there were not enough Capac Incas to fill the new posts that became necessary. So Pachacuti created an additional class of nobles, the Hahua (HAH-wah) Incas, "Incas by adoption or privilege." The Hahua Incas were men who had proved their loyalty during the Chanca war or had performed other valuable services for Pachacuti. Their male descendants inherited the rank of Hahua Incas. These noblemen held many administrative jobs throughout the empire.

Like the Sapa Inca, both Capac Incas and Hahua Incas were

*This silver figure represents an Inca noble. His earlobes have been stretched by large ear spools, which only Capac Incas and Hahua Incas were allowed to wear.*

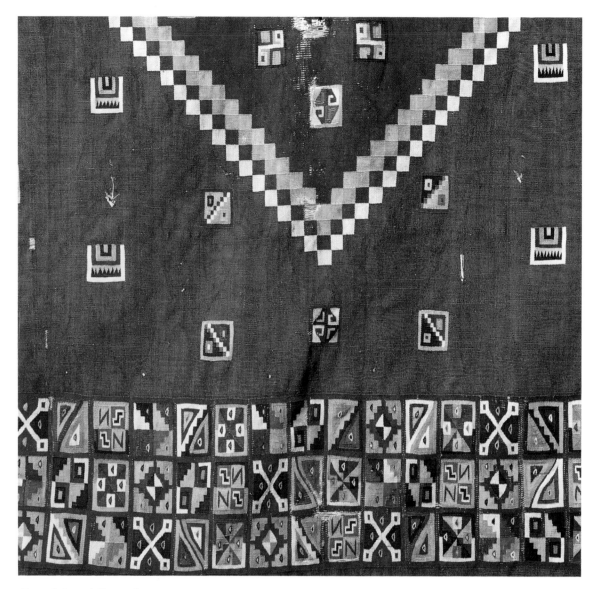

*One of the privileges that Inca nobles enjoyed was the right to wear garments made from* cumbi *cloth.*

entitled to wear ear spools. Both could have more than one wife, although the number of extra wives was under the Sapa Inca's control. Capac Incas and Hahua Incas could sometimes share other royal privileges, including the right to wear *cumbi* garments, the right to sit on a low stool (instead of the ground), the right to ride in a litter, and the right to marry a half-sister. Only Capac Incas could live in central Cuzco and hold the empire's most important positions.

## The Emperor's Agents

To rule Tahuantinsuyu effectively, the Sapa Inca had a highly organized government, although some of its details are unclear to us today. He delegated his authority to trusted nobles, beginning with his supreme council. This was made up of four officials who represented the four quarters of the empire. Next in importance were the provincial governors, who lived in their provinces and were responsible to the emperor alone.

Also under the direct orders of the Sapa Inca were inspectors called *tocoyricocs* (toh-koy-REE-kohks), "visitors." These were nobles who periodically traveled through the provinces to see that both officials and common citizens were living according to the emperor's decrees. Some *tocoyricocs* seem to have been specialists in various areas of administration. They collected tribute, made sure that storehouses were full, judged and punished crimes, double-checked quipu records, and supervised road and bridge construction and maintenance. *Tocoyricocs* reported their findings directly to the Sapa Inca.

## Native Chiefs

At the next level of society were the *curacas* (ku-RAH-kahs). These were the chiefs or leaders of peoples conquered by the Incas. So long as they remained loyal to the Sapa Inca, they were allowed to keep some of their wealth and authority. In return they had the responsibility of providing men from their communities to serve in the Inca army or to work on such things as building projects for the Incas.

*Curacas* were in charge of communities of anywhere from one hundred to ten thousand people. The more important *curacas* enjoyed many of the same privileges as Capac Incas and Hahua Incas, including riding in a litter and having more than one wife. And, like the nobles, *curacas* were expected to make lavish presents to the Sapa Inca, who gave them valuable presents in return.

The sons of *curacas* were sent to the same school in Cuzco where noble Inca boys were educated. (It was the only school in the empire.) This was a two-edged privilege, however. In Cuzco the *curacas'* sons were taught to think and believe as the Incas did. They were constantly observed, for the Sapa Inca had the right to

*This Chimú burial mask of gold and turquoise represented a chief's status and power. Chiefs from Chimor and other conquered areas became part of the Inca system of government as* curacas.

choose each *curaca's* successor. And with their sons so much in the Incas' power, the *curacas'* loyalty was almost guaranteed.

## HOSTAGE *HUACAS*

The Incas could be quite ingenious in finding ways to keep their subjects loyal. For example, whenever they conquered another tribe or nation, they took their new subjects' most important religious objects or statues back to Cuzco. There these *huacas* were carefully looked after and were worshiped as they would have been in their own lands. But they were also in the Incas' power—and very few peoples would dare to rebel against the empire that possessed their most sacred *huacas*.

## Colonists

Holding the sons of local rulers hostage was not the Incas' only means of keeping peace in their empire. One of their main ways of doing this was through a program of resettlement and colonization. Whenever the Incas conquered a new territory, they moved out any portion of the local population that was likely to cause trouble. These people were resettled in an area where loyalty to the Incas was well established. They were replaced by a group of dependable colonists, usually commoners, called *mitimas* (mee-TEE-mahs).

*Mitimas* were responsible for setting a good example of Inca citizenship. They were also entrusted with teaching conquered peoples Quechua, which Pachacuti had made the official language of the empire. And they were expected to put down any rebellions in their new territory.

Sometimes *mitimas* were sent to unpopulated areas. They might be settled near a new road or bridge, which they became responsible for maintaining. Or they might be given the task of farming land that had never been farmed before. Other *mitimas* were established in settlements along the empire's borders, which they were expected to protect.

*Mitimas* might be relocated hundreds of miles from their original homes. Sometimes thousands of people—even whole communities—were resettled together. They had no choice in the matter, but they were granted certain special privileges in recognition of their service to the empire. They were also allowed to keep their own unique customs and styles of clothing. In all other matters they were supposed to follow the way of life of their new territory and to obey its *curaca*.

## The Common People

Both before and during Inca times, the basic unit of social organization in the Andes was the *ayllu* (I-yoo). This was a group of related families who lived together in a defined area and shared land, crops, and animals. An *ayllu* could be quite small, or it could be as large as a whole town.

Although Inca nobles and city dwellers all belonged to *ayllus,* these groups were probably most important to the common people of Tahuantinsuyu. They lived in the countryside, their lives for the most part centered on farming and herding. Every autumn the local *curaca* divided up the land granted for the *ayllu's* use. Each householder, or married man, received a certain amount of land; this allotment increased or decreased along with the size of his family. If a householder was unable to work his land for some reason—if he was sick or injured, for example, or if he was away at war—other members of the *ayllu* worked it for him and made sure his family was provided for.

*The Incas decreed that the people of each province must wear headgear different from that worn in other provinces. Government officials needed only to look at a person's headdress to know where that person was from. This wool and cotton hat from eighth-century Peru may be similar to headgear worn in some parts of Tahuantinsuyu.*

### Farming for the Emperor and the Sun

The Inca government guaranteed that every household and *ayllu* would have enough land to raise all its own food. However, each area's farmland was divided into three parts: one for the Sun, one for the Sapa Inca, and one for the community. The peasants were required to work on all three, and they could tend their own allotments only after tending the Sun's and the Sapa Inca's.

The lands of the Sun were devoted to growing the crops necessary for religious uses, especially for sacrifices. These lands also provided food for all of the empire's priests, priestesses, and others in religious service. Cultivating the Sun's lands was one of the most important religious duties of the commoners. They sang hymns to the deities as they worked and never even walked across the fields without saying a reverent prayer.

The crops grown on the Sapa Inca's lands fed the royal family, the nobles, and everyone else in the service of the government. Large amounts of this produce also went into storehouses all over the empire. These supplied food to Inca armies on the march, travelers on government business, and the like. Food from the emperor's storehouses was also given to widows, the poor, and communities suffering from crop failures or other hardships. When the people worked on the Sapa Inca's lands, they sang songs in his praise.

### The Work Tax

In addition to cultivating the lands of the Sun and the Sapa Inca, common householders were required to provide other kinds of labor for the government. This part-time service, called *mit'a* (MEE-tah), could include such things as working in the mines, working as servants to the nobles, and transporting goods from place to place. A major form of *mit'a* was participation in public works projects: building temples, palaces, fortresses, roads, canals, agricultural terraces, and the like. The *mit'a* system was also used to recruit soldiers for the army.

Some communities had specific forms of *mit'a* permanently assigned to them. One village sent men to serve as dancers to entertain the Sapa Inca, and there were two tribes whose men carried the emperor's litter. Another tribe provided doctors for the royal family and nobility. Men of the Cañari (kah-NYAH-ree) region of Ecuador served in the Sapa Inca's personal guard. Communities located near bridges performed their *mit'a* by maintaining the bridges.

Sometimes *mit'a* took the form of providing certain goods for the Sapa Inca and nobles. Such goods included feathers, fish, seashells, wood, and other raw materials. The emperor demanded these things only of communities that could easily obtain them. There is even a story of one tribe that was so poor that the Sapa Inca required it to send him nothing but lice—apparently the only thing they had plenty of.

Skilled potters, woodworkers, goldsmiths, and other artisans were usually exempt from *mit'a*. Instead they gave everything they made to the Sapa Inca and nobles, who provided them with all their tools and materials. Similarly, *mit'a* was not required from architects, engineers, judges, *quipu-camayocs*, and others who worked directly for the government.

## Women's Work

Women were not expected to perform *mit'a*. But every common family was required to weave one garment a year for the government storehouses, and this weaving was usually done by the women. In addition, a wife sometimes accompanied her husband when he went away on his *mit'a* assignment; she cooked for him, carried loads for him, and assisted him in other ways.

*A husband and wife in the rural Andes work together to prepare the fields for planting in the same way that their Inca ancestors did.*

Women often worked in the fields with the men, especially at harvest and sowing time. Teamwork was essential to prepare the ground for planting. The men used a foot plow called a *taclla* (TAHK-yah) to turn the soil as they walked backward over the fields. Their wives, facing them, followed with a short-handled hoe called a *lampa*, which they used to break up clods of earth.

Women's main tasks were child care, cooking, housekeeping, and making cloth. (Even noblewomen spent a great deal of time spinning and weaving, and they were responsible for the smooth running of their households.) The inspectors who periodically toured the empire checked to make sure that women were doing these things satisfactorily. If the inspector felt that a woman did not keep her house clean enough, he punished her by making her eat dirt in front of the whole community.

The husbands and wives of the common people were selected for them by the *curacas*, who probably honored choices already made by couples or their parents. A commoner was allowed to have only one wife, and marriage was for life. A man who turned his wife out of his house was severely punished. If his wife died, a year or two later the *curaca* usually gave him a new wife. If a woman's husband died, she generally remained a widow. She was provided for by her *ayllu* and the government. In return, she was given the responsibility of raising one or more orphans.

## The Chosen Women

Most women spent their entire lives in their *ayllus,* but there was one major exception. Every year a government official traveled to all the villages of each province. He selected the prettiest, pleasantest, and most talented nine- and ten-year-old girls to go to the provincial capital for special training. These girls were the *acllas* (AHK-yahs), "chosen women." They lived in a kind of convent called the *Acllahuasi* (AHK-yah-WAH-see), where they learned to prepare the best quality *chicha*, to cook the finest food, and to dye, spin, and weave cotton and wool to the highest standard. They were also thoroughly educated in religion.

The *acllas'* training lasted three or four years. At the end of this time they were taken to Cuzco and brought before the Sapa Inca, who decided their futures. The emperor chose the most beautiful girls to become his own concubines. He gave others to nobles and *curacas* whom he wished to reward or honor. Some acllas were set aside to be sacrificed in impor-

# IF YOU LIVED IN TAHUANTINSUYU

If you had been born in the Inca Empire, your way of life would have been determined by the facts of your birth—whether you were a girl or a boy, a noble or a commoner. With this chart you can trace the course your life might have taken as a commoner in the Andean countryside.

## You were born in a small village . . . .

### As a Boy . . .                                            As a Girl . . .

As a baby, you are carried everywhere with your mother, riding in a blanket tied to her back. She nurses you three times a day. When you are weaned, around age two, your hair is cut for the first time in a special ceremony and you are given your childhood name. As soon as you can walk, you begin to help your parents with small chores. Sometimes when they are working you are put in a chest-high, cloth-lined pit in the ground with a few toys to play with.

**At age 5,** you spend most of your time with your father, helping him with his tasks. You have some time to play with such toys as balls and tops.

**From about age 9,** you work most of the time, herding llamas and alpacas, killing small birds, gathering firewood, and helping in the fields.

**Around age 14,** in a public ceremony, you are given your breechcloth, which has been specially woven for you by your mother. Wearing this garment means that you are now a man, and you are given your permanent name. You continue to live with your parents and help your father with his work.

**By the age of 25,** you must be married. Your wife is chosen for you from your *ayllu* by your *curaca*. You and your wife move into your own house. You are now required to perform *mit'a;* your work service will be assigned to you by the *curaca*. Otherwise you spend most of your time working in the fields.

**At about age 50,** you are released from the *mit'a* requirement. Your needs are supplied by your *ayllu* and by the government. In return you are expected to perform light tasks such as collecting grass for use as thatch and other purposes, making ropes, looking after animals, and teaching children. You are highly respected for your experience and wisdom.

**At age 5** you spend most of your time with your mother, helping her with her tasks. You have some time to play with such toys as balls, tops, and rag dolls.

**From about age 9,** you work most of the time, spinning thread, gathering plants for use as dyes and medicines, gathering firewood, helping prepare food, helping to care for your younger brothers and sisters, and sometimes herding animals and helping in the fields.

**Around age 14,** your family holds a ceremony to celebrate your becoming a woman, and you receive your permanent name. You continue to live at home and help your mother with her work.

**Between the ages of 16 and 20,** you get married. Your husband is chosen for you from your *ayllu* by your *curaca*. You and your husband move into your own house. You spend most of your time taking care of your children, cooking, and making cloth, and you also work in the fields. Whenever your hands are not busy with something else, you are spinning.

**From about age 50,** your needs are supplied by your *ayllu* and the government. In return you are expected to perform only light household chores and to help teach the young. You are highly respected for your experience and wisdom.

When you die your body is buried along with many of your possessions. At your funeral your relatives wear black, sing laments, do mournful dances, and tell stories about your life.

*Overseen by a* mamacuna, Acllas *spin thread in this drawing by Huaman Poma.*

tant religious rituals. The rest became *mamacunas* (MAH-mah-KU-nahs), the most respected and privileged women in Tahuantinsuyu.

*Mamacunas* were the teachers of the *acllas*. They also served as priestesses and attendants in the empire's temples and shrines. They were often called the Brides of the Sun, for they were symbolically married to Inti, or sometimes to other gods. They were not allowed to have any relationships with human men other then the Sapa Inca.

The *mamacunas* took part in rituals and had other religious duties, such as interpreting the will of the deities and foretelling the future. They were also responsible for preparing the food and drink that was used in rituals, and they cooked the priests' meals. One of their major duties was making *cumbi* cloth, which was worn by the emperor, used to adorn statues of the deities, and burned (in great quantities) as a sacrifice.

## Time to Celebrate

The Sapa Inca controlled his empire largely by making certain that his subjects were always busy—laziness was one of the most serious of crimes in Tahuantinsuyu. Even so, not every day was a working day. Each month there were at least three feast days, and usually a major festival that lasted for roughly a week.

Feasts were held to celebrate marriages, young people's coming of age, and other special occasions. There was a festival to honor the dead. Many of the holidays were related to agricultural work, such as planting and harvesting the crops. The most important festivals were at the winter and summer solstices.

All festivals began with religious ceremonies and sacrifices. Then there was eating and drinking, storytelling and singing, music and dancing—often lasting for days. In these celebrations,

both solemn and joyous, the people honored their deities and their ruler, and temporarily forgot their burdens. And by providing these holidays, the Son of the Sun bound his empire together in both work and play.

*Inti Raymi, the Feast of the Sun, was the Incas' great annual celebration of the winter solstice. This holiday is still celebrated in Cuzco every June 24, when the Incas' descendants remember and re-create the splendor of Tahuantinsuyu.*

# HARDSHIP, CHANGE, AND SURVIVAL

**CHAPTER FIVE**

*The Roman Catholic feast of Corpus Christi is an occasion for parades and pageantry in Cuzco, much as the great feasts of the Incas were. Andean and European traditions mingle, as demonstrated by this Peruvian musician marching in a Corpus Christi parade.*

The Spanish conquest was a disaster for the people of Tahuantinsuyu. The conquistadores took over Inca institutions such as *mitimas* and *mit'a,* but they took no care to ensure the welfare and contentment of the workers. In fact, they virtually enslaved the people. Untold numbers died from the hardships of forced labor, especially in the gold and silver mines. Still more died of smallpox, measles, and other European diseases. Fifty years after the conquest, it is estimated, there were only 500,000 people left of the seven million subjects of the Inca Empire. Yet despite all obstacles, these survivors and their descendants preserved much of the Inca heritage, which lives on to this day.

## The Inca Resistance

When Francisco Pizarro took over the government in Cuzco, he was afraid that nobles and *curacas* would form their own states and rebel against Spanish rule. So in March of 1534 he set up Huayna Capac's son Manco II as Sapa Inca, even allowing him the full coronation ceremonies. But Manco was a puppet ruler, and Pizarro was pulling the strings.

For a while Manco was obedient to his Spanish masters. Then Pizarro left Cuzco to found Lima (LEE-muh), today Peru's capital, and other conquistadores went off to explore and subdue

the rest of Tahuantinsuyu. Those who remained abused Manco and his wives. At the same time, Manco received ever more reports of his people's mistreatment at the hands of Spanish treasure seekers, who had been pouring into the empire in large numbers since the conquest.

In April of 1536 Manco left Cuzco, pretending that he was fetching a life-size golden statue for the conquistadores. Instead he came back at the head of an army, which he had secretly raised with the help of the high priest of Coricancha. They attacked and burned Cuzco, then besieged the city for a year.

*The curved wall at the right in this picture was originally part of Coricancha, Tahuantinsuyu's most important temple. Spanish colonists built a church and monastery on top of the Inca holy place. When an earthquake shook Cuzco in 1950, the Spanish structure was severely damaged, but the Inca stonework survived intact.*

### Empire in Exile

When the Spaniards at last managed to capture Sacsahuamán, the rebel headquarters, Manco and his followers withdrew to the jungle of Vilcabamba (VEEL-kah-BAHM-bah), northwest of Cuzco. In this wild and inaccessible place Manco set up a new

Inca state. His warriors continued to attack the Spaniards at every opportunity.

Manco held out until 1545, when he was murdered by a group of Spanish deserters whom he had befriended. His young son Sayri Tupac (SY-ree TOO-pak) succeeded him as ruler of Vilcabamba, but went over to the conquistadores thirteen years later. Another son, Titu Cusi (TEE-too KOO-see), renewed the war against the Spaniards. Eventually he began negotiating with them; by always seeming to be just about to give up, he kept Vilcabamba safe until his death in 1571.

Titu Cusi's brother and successor, Tupac Amaru (ah-MAH-roo), was not so lucky. The new Spanish governor of Peru had vowed to destroy Vilcabamba and the last remains of Inca power. In 1572 he was successful. As Vilcabamba burned, Tupac Amaru fled into the rain forest, where Spanish soldiers eventually captured him. They took him back to Cuzco in chains. In the main square, where generations of Incas had held their sacrifices and celebrations, Tupac Amaru, the last Son of the Sun, was beheaded.

## A NAME TO BE RECKONED WITH

In the century following Tupac Amaru's execution, Spanish rule in western South America received no serious challenges. Then in 1780 a descendant of Tupac Amaru, José Gabriel Condorcanqui, took the name of Tupac Amaru II and led the native people of Peru in an uprising against the colonial government. His rebellion eventually spread all the way from Cuzco to Argentina and was nearly successful. Finally in 1782, with dreadful cruelty, the authorities crushed the revolt. Like his ancestor, Tupac Amaru II was executed in Cuzco's Plaza de Armas. But his heroism was never forgotten by his people, and in the 1970s the government of Peru adopted his image as a symbol of social reform.

## Spanish Colonies

With the conquest of Vilcabamba, all of the lands that had made up Tahuantinsuyu were under Spanish control. By this time there were few remnants of Inca splendor. The emperor's storehouses had long ago been completely looted. Nearly all of the beautifully crafted gold and silver items that had filled the empire's temples and palaces had been melted down and shipped to Spain in the form of ingots. Thousands of quipus had been burned. Even most of the mummies of the Sapa Incas and their Coyas had been destroyed.

## The Conquistadores' Cuzco

Cuzco, "the navel of the world," was being transformed into a colonial city. The conquistadores had taken over Inca palaces or had had new mansions built for themselves—often out of stones removed from Inca buildings. A church and monastery had been constructed on the foundations of Coricancha. The Holy Plaza (Huacapata) was now the Plaza of War (Plaza de Armas), and a cathedral was being built on its east side. Close to the cathedral was a smaller church, erected on the site of the Incas' main temple of Viracocha.

*Cuzco's cathedral dominates the east side of the Plaza de Armas, where many of the Incas' most important ceremonies were once held.*

Many more churches, monasteries, and convents were built through-out greater Cuzco during the next hundred years. Nevertheless, the Incas' Cuzco was not completely erased. A number of the Spanish buildings incorporated Inca foundations and walls. For example, the convent of Santa Catalina used one of the walls of the Acllahuasi in its exterior. And when strong earthquakes shook Cuzco in 1650 and again in 1950, the remaining Inca stonework stood fast, while many of the Spanish structures crumbled and had to be rebuilt.

## Hard Times

The conquistadores and most of the landowners and local officials who followed them lived like princes at the expense of the native people. Many Spaniards, in both Europe and South America, protested against the mistreatment of the natives. But it did little good, even when the king of Spain passed laws designed to protect them. Greed was the supreme power in the Spanish colonies.

The new rulers demanded even more and heavier labor than the Sapa Inca had. They did not provide frequent holidays, relief during hard times, or any of the other humane benefits of the Inca system. They exploited both the land and the people to mine as many precious metals as possible. Underfed and overworked miners and pack bearers were often given nothing but coca leaves to keep them going.

To escape such fates, large numbers of the natives moved into isolated places in the highlands, where, in many ways, their lives continued as always. But they remained illiterate, politically powerless, and practically landless, while small Spanish elites controlled government, education, religion, and the military. When the colonies won independence from Spain in the nineteenth century, the situation barely improved. Only in the twentieth century have the native majorities of the Incas' former lands begun to enjoy political rights, economic improvements, and respect for their culture.

## The New Religion

When the Spanish brought their rule to South America, they brought their religion as well. Indeed, the zeal for spreading the Roman Catholic faith was one of the major forces behind the conquest. Missionary priests flocked to Peru almost as eagerly as treasure seekers did.

The missionaries wanted to completely stamp out the religion of Tahuantinsuyu. But there were many Andean beliefs and practices that could not be destroyed and have survived in various forms to the present. For instance, on the Catholic feast of Corpus Christi beautifully dressed statues of various saints are taken out of their churches in and around Cuzco with great pageantry. They are all brought together in the main square, just as all of the Incas' religious statues were brought out for the great festivals of Tahuantinsuyu.

Some Inca beliefs and practices were very similar to Catholic ones, such as the

*Our Lady of Pomata was painted by an artist of the Cuzco school in the first half of the eighteenth century.*

## THE CUZCO SCHOOL OF PAINTING

From the time of Pachacuti, scenes of Inca history were painted on boards that were kept in Coricancha. After the Spanish conquest, Inca art styles and traditions combined with European ones. The result was what is called the Cuzco school of painting, which flourished in the seventeenth and eighteenth centuries.

The artists of the Cuzco school were mostly of mixed Spanish and native heritage. All of them were Roman Catholics and used their art to teach and explain the new religion. Their paintings hung on the walls of churches and convents not only in Cuzco but throughout the Spanish colonies of the Americas.

In the art of the Cuzco school, saints and biblical figures sometimes appear in Andean clothing. But whether the people in these paintings are dressed in native or European style, their costumes are elaborately detailed, brightly colored, and lavished with gold. Clearly the Incas' love of splendid cloth lived on in the artists of the Cuzco school.

belief in a creator god who was the ultimate source of everything. Similarly, the Inca practice of confession was easily converted to the Catholic rite of confessing sins to a priest. And just as the Incas had *mamacunas* set aside from the rest of society for religious service, the Catholic church had nuns.

Other aspects of Inca religion have continued to exist alongside the new faith with little or no adaptation. Mountains, especially snow-capped ones, are still revered. Illnesses are often treated with magical charms and herbs. Prayers and offerings are made to Pacha-mama, Mother Earth. And on the Island of the Sun in Lake Titicaca, there is an elaborate festival every year at planting time, with music and dancing; feasting and drinking of *chicha;* prayers against frost, hail, and lightning; and the sacrifice of a white llama.

## Living Traditions

In Peru, Bolivia, and Ecuador today there are many living legacies of the Incas, especially in the rural highlands. For millions of people in these areas, the major or only language is Quechua, the official language of Tahuantinsuyu. Their communities continue to be organized along the lines of the ancient *ayllus*. Many still think of the world as being divided into four quarters.

Each region has its own distinctive headgear, just as in Inca days, when the emperors decreed different headdresses for every rank and every province. Many men wear the old poncho-style tunics, although usually with shirts and trousers underneath. Women's shawls are often shorter versions of the mantles that Inca women wore over their shoulders; simple *tupu* pins are still used to fasten them.

Most of these clothes are homemade in the old way. Women spin with drop spindles as they are walking along, carrying their babies on their backs in handwoven blankets. Weaving continues to be done on backstrap looms; the bright colors and patterns of the cloth recall Inca traditions of weaving. Pottery and other crafts also show the Inca influence.

Many rural houses are no different from those of the commoners of Tahuantinsuyu: one-room dwellings with dirt floors, thatched roofs, and doorways facing east to greet the rising sun. Meals are often cooked on small clay stoves fueled by llama dung, just as in Inca times. Modern highlanders eat the same foods as their ancestors, too. Potatoes are the

*A woman in Cuzco weaves cloth much as her Inca foremothers did.*

mainstay of the diet; soups and stews are thickened with quinoa; and guinea-pig meat (or, more rarely, llama meat) is enjoyed on special occasions.

In many places farming methods have not changed since the Sons of the Sun reigned. A number of agricultural terraces and irrigation canals have remained in use, and many that had fallen into disuse are being repaired and reclaimed. Boys and girls herd llamas and alpacas in the high grasslands; sheep, introduced by the Spanish, are now included in the flocks, too. Community leaders sometimes use simple quipus to keep track of livestock and crop yields.

Music has remained important in Andean life through the centuries. European instruments such as guitars are now common, but so are native instruments. These include various kinds of flutes and drums, conch-shell trumpets, and panpipes of all sizes. Traditional Andean music uses a five-note scale and has a haunting, unforgettable quality. Many traditional dances have been kept alive as well.

Music, dancing, gorgeous costumes, and pageantry are main

*A Bolivian man playing the panpipes*

features of Cuzco's modern celebration of Inti Raymi, the Incas' great Feast of the Sun. This festival is now held in the ruins of Sacsahuamán every June 24. Many other Andean communities have their own Inti Raymi festivals, where villagers reenact the defeat of the last Inca emperor. But in this version, the Son of the Sun's death is only a temporary eclipse. One day, they say, he will return to life and bring back the power and splendor of Tahuantinsuyu.

## Rediscovering the Incas

The legacy of the Incas has reached far beyond their own land. To start with, it could be said that much of European history would not have occurred without them. When the conquistadores seized the riches of Tahuantinsuyu, they melted down the precious metals and sent them back to their king. He and his successors used this wealth to finance wars, building projects, works of art, and more. In short, the Spanish empire of the sixteenth century was largely built on the wealth of the Inca empire.

### Tales of an Exotic Land

Europeans were fascinated by everything they heard about the Incas. Spanish soldiers, officials, and priests in the sixteenth and seventeenth centuries wrote many books to satisfy this interest. A particularly intriguing account of Inca culture and history was published in Lisbon, Portugal, in 1609. It was by Garcilaso de la Vega, the son of a conquistador and an Inca *ñusta*. This is sometimes called the first work of Peruvian literature, although it was written in Spain, where Garcilaso lived from around age twenty until his death in 1616.

In the eighteenth century many authors wrote popular plays and novels inspired by stories of the Incas, their empire, and their fabulous wealth. The most famous of these is the French writer

## THE LAST INCA BRIDGE

In the early 1970s journalist Loren McIntyre and his wife, Sue, were exploring some way south of Cuzco along the Apurimac River. To their amazement they found an Inca-style suspension bridge spanning the river gorge. As they were about to try crossing it, they were stopped by a villager named Luis Choqueneira, who warned them that the bridge was dying. He went on to tell them that he was one of the *chaca camayocs,* the bridge keepers. They rebuilt the bridge every year, just as Topa Yupanqui had ordered their ancestors to do five centuries earlier.

The McIntyres accepted Luis Choqueneira's invitation to come see the rebuilding of the bridge. On the appointed day the people of two villages gathered by the river, their hats decorated with flowers, and set to work. Everyone helped: Children pounded bundles of tough grass, which the women then spun into cords. The men had brought 22,000 feet of thick, handspun rope, which they braided into six cables.

The next day a hundred men and boys hung the one-hundred-foot-long bridge across the gorge. On the third day three elderly bridge keepers completed the bridge by weaving together twigs to make a footing. During the whole project, coca leaves and ears of maize were burned as offerings at the bridge's foundations. Loren McIntyre said that he and his wife felt as if they "had been transported back to the days when the sun of the Incas stood at zenith."

Voltaire's satirical novel *Candide*. Books of this period tended to portray the Incas as "noble savages," a popular image of native peoples at that time.

In the 1840s American William Prescott's well-researched *Conquest of Peru* awakened serious historical interest in the Incas. At the same time Prescott's book presented the fall of Tahuantinsuyu as an epic tale of adventure and tragedy. It has enthralled readers for generations.

*Peruvian villagers cross the rope suspension bridge they have just constructed using the same methods that were employed by their ancestors in Inca times.*

### The Lost City

One of Prescott's readers was a young American named Hiram Bingham. In 1911 Bingham set out on an expedition to search for the Incas' last capital in Vilcabamba. What he found in the jungle was even more spectacular: Machu Picchu (MAH-choo PEE-choo), the best preserved Inca city yet rediscovered.

*Machu Picchu, the mysterious "lost city" that has awed and inspired millions of visitors with its magnificent stonework and breathtaking setting*

Machu Picchu is perched on a ridge overlooking the Urubamba River. The city's buildings and terraces blend harmoniously with the spectacular setting. The architecture and stonework are of the best quality, probably dating from the reign of Pachacuti. But no one knows for certain why the Sapa Inca had Machu Picchu built. It may have been a royal retreat, a regional ceremonial center, or one of a series of agricultural settlements. Or, since most of the bodies in the cemetery were found to be female, perhaps Machu Picchu was at some point a refuge for *acllas* and *mamacunas*.

Hiram Bingham's books about Machu Picchu—and the mysterious "lost city" itself—excited worldwide interest in the Incas. Every year now thousands of people travel to Peru to visit Machu Picchu, Cuzco, and other Inca sites, making tourism one of Peru's leading industries. And visitors to these great stone cities in the Andes seldom come away unmoved by the magnificence of the Incas' achievements.

## Feeding the World

The Incas' greatest legacy to the world today is far humbler than palaces and temples, and far more valuable than all the empire's gold and silver together. It is the potato, whose cultivation was perfected by the Incas and which is now a major food for people all over the globe. The Incas have given us other important crops as well, including many kinds of beans, peppers, and squash.

Some Inca foods are just now starting to appear in markets and on dinner tables outside the Andes; chief among these is quinoa, which is much richer in protein than wheat. Many Inca crops contribute to the breeding of improved varieties of plants for farms and gardens everywhere. And in the United States and other countries, Inca farming methods are being studied to learn ways to improve agriculture, especially irrigation and erosion control. We already owe much of the world's food supply to the Incas, and in the future we are likely to owe them even more.

*The Incas grew more than two hundred varieties of potato. The humble tubers are Tahuantinsuyu's greatest gift to the world, feeding billions of people every year.*

# The Incas: A Chronology*

| | |
|---|---|
| **1200** | Founding of Cuzco |
| **1200–1438** | Reigns of Manco Capac, Sinchi Roca, Lloqui Yupanqui, Mayta Capac, Capac Yupanqui, Inca Roca, Yahuar Huaca, and Viracocha |
| **1438** | War against the Chancas |
| **1438–1471** | Reign of Pachacuti |
| **between 1465 & 1470** | Topa Yupanqui conquers Chimor |
| **1471–1493** | Reign of Topa Yupanqui |
| **1493–1527** | Reign of Huayna Capac |
| **1527** | Francisco Pizarro lands at Tumbes, soon departs; epidemic kills 200,000 people, including Huayna Capac |
| **1527–1532** | Civil war between Huascar and Atahualpa; Atahualpa victorious |
| **November 16, 1532** | Spaniards commanded by Francisco Pizarro ambush and capture Atahualpa |
| **July 1533** | Execution of Atahualpa |
| **November 15, 1533** | Spaniards take over Cuzco |
| **March 1534** | Pizarro has Manco II crowned as Sapa Inca |
| **April 1536** | Manco rebels against the Spanish, attacks and besieges Cuzco |
| **1537** | Manco establishes new Inca state in Vilcabamba |
| **1545** | Murder of Manco II; succeeded by Sayri Tupac |
| **1558** | Sayri Tupac goes over to the Spanish |
| **1558–1571** | Titu Cusi rules in Vilcabamba |
| **1571** | Tupac Amaru succeeds Titu Cusi |
| **1572** | Spanish governor conquers Vilcabamba; Tupac Amaru is captured and beheaded |

*All dates before 1532 are approximate.

# GLOSSARY

**aclla** (AHK-yah): "chosen woman"; a girl selected for special training in religion and fine weaving and cooking

**Acllahuasi** (AHK-yah-WAH-see): "House of the Chosen Women"; a building where *mamacunas* lived and taught the *acllas*. Every provincial capital had an *acllahuasi;* the one in Cuzco, located near Coricancha, housed at least fifteen hundred girls and women.

**adobe** (uh-DOH-bee): brick made of sun-dried mud and straw

**amautas** (ah-MOW-tahs): "wise men"; elderly men who composed and preserved dramas, poems, and stories. They also educated the sons of the nobles.

**archaeologist:** a person who studies the remains—such as pottery, buildings, and works of art—of past human cultures

**artisan:** an expert in a craft, such as a goldsmith, potter, woodworker, or weaver

**ayllu** (I-yoo): a group of related families who lived in a defined area and shared land, crops, and animals

**bola:** a long cord with weights attached at the ends, thrown to entangle the legs of an enemy warrior or a hunted animal

**Capac Incas:** the highest-ranking nobles, who traced their ancestry directly back to the legendary first Inca

**charqui** (CHAR-kee): dried strips of llama or alpaca meat

**chasquis** (CHAHS-kees): runners posted at stations along the roads to relay messages through the empire

**chicha** (CHEE-chah): an alcoholic drink usually made from fermented maize; corn beer

**chuño** (CHOO-nyoh): freeze-dried potatoes

**coca:** a shrub native to the jungles of the eastern slopes of the Andes; the source of cocaine. Its leaves were used in Inca religious rituals.

**concubine:** a secondary wife; a legally recognized mistress

**conquistadores** (kahn-KEES-tuh-DOR-ays): the Spanish word for "conquerors"; it refers especially to the Spaniards who conquered Mexico and Peru in the sixteenth century.

**Coricancha** (koh-ree-KAHN-chah): "Golden Enclosure"; the Inca empire's main temple, in which there were shrines for all the major deities

**Coya:** the principal wife of the Inca ruler; the queen or empress

*cumbi* (KUM-bee): elaborately patterned cloth woven of vicuña wool

*curaca* (ku-RAH-kah): the native leader of a tribe, nation, or smaller community under Inca rule

**divination:** the art of discovering hidden facts about the past, present, or future. The Inca priests and priestesses who heard confessions practiced divination by casting small stones and interpreting the pattern in which they fell, or by interpreting the condition of a sacrificed animal's internal organs.

**Hahua** (HAH-wah) **Incas:** "Incas by adoption or privilege"; the second rank of Inca nobles

*huaca* (WAH-kah): a person, place, or object believed to contain divine power

*kero* (KEH-roh): a wide-mouthed cup carved out of wood, large enough to hold one or two quarts of *chicha*

**litter:** a kind of enclosed couch mounted on horizontal poles for carrying one or two people

*mamacunas* (MAH-mah-KU-nahs): women selected for various kinds of religious service, including teaching the *acllas*

**missionary:** a person who travels to a far-off place to teach his or her religion to the people of that place

*mit'a* (MEE-tah): work service; part-time work on government projects and the like, required of all male commoners. The word literally means "a turn" in Quechua.

*mitimas* (mee-TEE-mahs): colonists; people sent in groups to settle in new areas of the empire

*mocha* (MOH-chah): a gesture of reverence made to deities, *huacas,* the emperor, and nobles

**myth:** a sacred story; a story that explains or describes the religious beliefs of a people

*ñusta* (NYOOS-tah): a girl or unmarried woman belonging to the highest nobility

*palla* (PAH-yah): a married woman belonging to the highest nobility

*panaca* (pah-NAH-kah): a group made up of all the direct descendants of a dead emperor, excluding the son who succeeded as ruler. The *panaca* inherited all of the emperor's wealth and was responsible for caring for his mummy and preserving songs and stories of his deeds.

**Quechua** (KESH-wah): a people who lived north of Cuzco and became allies of the Incas under the emperor Viracocha. Also, their language, which became the official language of the Inca empire. It is still spoken by millions of people in Ecuador, Peru, and Bolivia.

**quinoa** (KEEN-wah): a plant native to the Andean highlands. Its nutty-tasting grainlike seeds have been a staple food in the region since before Inca times.

**quipu** (KEE-poo): a record-keeping device made of knotted cords

*quipucamayos* (KEE-poo-kah-MY-ohs): "quipu keepers"; men in charge of making and interpreting quipus

**ritual:** an action or series of actions done in a certain way for religious reasons; a religious ceremony

**Sapa Inca:** "unique or supreme Inca"; a title of the Inca emperor

*tocoyricoc* (toh-koy-REE-kohk): "he who sees all"; a traveling government inspector

*tupu* (TU-poo): a metal pin with a large head, used to fasten a woman's mantle or shawl

# FOR FURTHER READING

Baquedano, Elizabeth. *Aztec, Inca, and Maya.* New York: Knopf, 1993.

Beck, Barbara L. *The Incas.* rev. ed., 2d ed. New York: Franklin Watts, 1983.

Blassingame, Wyatt. *The Incas and the Spanish Conquest.* New York: J. Messner, 1980.

Chrisp, Peter. *The Incas.* New York: Thomson Learning, 1994.

Cohen, Daniel. *Hiram Bingham and the Dream of Gold.* New York: M. Evans, 1984.

Gemming, Elizabeth. *Lost City in the Clouds: The Discovery of Machu Picchu.* New York: Coward, McCann and Geohegan, 1980.

Gonzalez, Christina. *Inca Civilization.* Chicago: Childrens Press, 1993.

Karen, Ruth. *Kingdom of the Sun: The Inca, Empire Builders of the Americas.* New York: Four Winds Press, 1975.

Marrin, Albert. *Inca and Spaniard: Pizarro and the Conquest of Peru.* New York: Atheneum, 1989.

McKissack, Pat. *The Inca.* Chicago: Childrens Press, 1985.

McMullen, David. *Mystery in Peru: The Lines of Nazca.* New York: Contemporary Perspectives, 1977.

Morrison, Marion. *An Inca Farmer.* Vero Beach, Florida: Rourke Enterprises, 1988.

Neurath, Marie. *They Lived Like This in Ancient Peru.* New York: Franklin Watts, 1966.

Newman, Shirley. *The Incas.* New York: Franklin Watts, 1992.

Steele, Philip. *The Incas and Machu Picchu.* New York: Dillon Press, 1993.

von Hagen, Victor W. *The Incas: People of the Sun.* New York: World Publishing, 1961.

# BIBLIOGRAPHY

Beltran, Miriam. *Cuzco: Window on Peru.* 2d ed., rev. New York: Knopf, 1970.

Bingham, Hiram. *Lost City of the Incas: The Story of Machu Picchu and Its Builders.* 1948. Reprint, New York: Atheneum, 1963.

Cobo, Father Bernabe. *Inca Religion and Customs.* trans. Roland Hamilton. Austin: University of Texas Press, 1990.

Davies, Nigel. *The Incas.* Niwot: The University Press of Colorado, 1995.

Domenici, Viviano, and Davide Domenici. "Talking Knots of the Inka" in *Archaeology.* vol. 49, no. 6, November/December 1996. pp. 50–56.

Editors of Time-Life Books. *Incas: Lords of Gold and Glory.* Alexandria, Virginia: Time-Life Books, 1992.

Huaman Poma. *Letter to a King: A Peruvian Chief's Account of Life under the Incas and under Spanish Rule.* trans. Christopher Dilke. New York: Dutton, 1978.

Karen, Ruth. *Kingdom of the Sun: The Inca, Empire Builders of the Americas.* New York: Four Winds Press, 1975.

Kendall, Ann. *Everyday Life of the Incas.* New York: Putnam, 1973.

McIntyre, Loren. "The High Andes: South America's Islands in the Sky" in *National Geographic.* vol. 171, no. 4, April 1987. pp. 422–459.

McIntyre, Loren. *The Incredible Incas and Their Timeless Land.* Washington: National Geographic Society, 1975.

Prescott, William H. *History of the Conquest of Mexico and History of the Conquest of Peru.* 1843 & 1847. Reprint, New York: Modern Library, no date.

von Hagen, Victor W. *Realm of the Incas.* New York: Mentor Books, 1957.

# INDEX

*Page numbers for illustrations are in **boldface***

# ABOUT THE AUTHOR

Kathryn Hinds has been fascinated by cultures of the past for most of her life; as a child she dreamed of becoming an archaeologist or a writer. She grew up near Rochester, New York, then moved to New York City to study music and writing at Barnard College. She did graduate work in comparative literature at the City University of New York. For several years she has worked as a free-lance editor of children's books. She also writes poetry, which has been published in a number of magazines. Ms. Hinds now lives in the north Georgia mountains with her husband, their son, a cat, and a dog. Her other books in this series are *The Vikings, The Ancient Romans, The Celts of Northern Europe,* and *India's Gupta Dynasty.*